Baseball in the '50s

It's 1956 in Brooklyn's Ebbets Field as Jackie Robinson steals home safely against the crosstown rival, the New York Giants.

Baseball in the '50s

A Decade of Transition

An Illustrated History

Donald Honig

Crown Publishers, Inc.
New York

Published by Crown Publishers, Inc., 225 Park Avenue South, New York, New York, 10003
and represented in Canada by the Canadian MANDA Group

CROWN is a trademark of Crown Publishers, Inc.

Manufactured in the United States of America

Library of Congress Cataloging-in-Publication Data

Honig, Donald.
Baseball in the 50s.

Includes index.
1. Baseball—United States—History.   I. Title.
II. Title: Baseball in the fifties.
GV863.A1H67   1987   796.357'0973   87-5224

ISBN 0-517-56578-1

10 9 8 7 6 5 4 3 2 1

First Edition

Design: Robert Aulicino

For my daughter Catherine

By Donald Honig

Nonfiction

Baseball When the Grass Was Real
Baseball Between the Lines
The Man in the Dugout
The October Heroes
The Image of Their Greatness (with Lawrence Ritter)
The 100 Greatest Baseball Players of All Time (with Lawrence Ritter; Revised Edition)
The Brooklyn Dodgers: An Illustrated Tribute
The New York Yankees: An Illustrated History (Revised Edition)
Baseball's 10 Greatest Teams
The Los Angeles Dodgers: The First Quarter Century
The National League: An Illustrated History (Revised Edition)
The American League: An Illustrated History (Revised Edition)
The Boston Red Sox: An Illustrated Tribute
Baseball America
The New York Mets: The First Quarter Century (Revised Edition)
The World Series: An Illustrated History
Baseball in the '50s

Fiction

Sidewalk Caesar
Walk Like a Man
The Americans
Divide the Night
No Song to Sing
Judgment Night
The Love Thief
The Severith Style
Illusions
I Should Have Sold Petunias
The Last Great Season
Marching Home

Contents

Acknowledgments

I am deeply indebted to a great number of people for their generous assistance in photo research and in gathering the photographs reproduced in this book. Special thanks are due Michael P. Aronstein, president of Card Memorabilia Associates, Ltd., for his generosity and insights. Thanks also to Kip Ingle of the St. Louis Cardinals and to Brian Granger and Jon Braude of the Cincinnati Reds.

For their good advice, wise counsel, and steady encouragement, I am grateful to these keen students of baseball history: David Markson, Lawrence Ritter, Stanley Honig, Andrew Aronstein, Allan J. Grotheer, Douglas Mulcahey, Louis Kiefer, and Thomas Brookman.

Introduction

The 1950s were the Eisenhower years, a time of relative peace and calm. Falling between the end of World War II and the tumultuous manifestations of the 1960s, they have taken on an air of tranquility and nostalgia unique in America's twentieth-century experience, a sort of mid-century American Edwardian twilight.

For big-league baseball, the 1950s were vigorous and transitional. It was the decade of powerhouse teams like the Brooklyn Dodgers, the Milwaukee Braves, and most of all the New York Yankees: the imperial Yankees and their calculating buffoon of a manager, Casey Stengel. It was the decade that saw the retirement of quintessential heroes Bob Feller and Joe DiMaggio, stunning heroics by an aging Ted Williams, and the launching of the careers of Mickey Mantle, Willie Mays, Henry Aaron, and Roberto Clemente.

Overall, the proliferation of talent made this decade a match for any in the game's history, with the entrance upon the major-league rolls of players like Al Kaline, Brooks Robinson, Whitey Ford, Eddie Mathews, Ken Boyer, Frank Robinson, Sandy Koufax, Ernie Banks, Rocky Colavito, Orlando Cepeda, Herb Score, Bob Gibson, Don Drysdale, and many others. Some went on to careers that endured for decades; many were enshrined in the Hall of Fame.

But, of course, no decade, no year, no day of murmurous tranquility is without the rustling of its obverse side. Even as the nation was quietly flickering with vibrations that would prove explosive in a later decade, so was baseball beginning to change, reflecting, in its way, the alterations in the larger social fabric. Most notable was the steady, team-by-team crashing of color barriers, spearheaded by Jackie Robinson a few years before, as baseball's own social revolution furthered itself and became final and irreversible.

At first the changes caused little more than a murmur. The first franchise shifts in half a century occurred—the Boston Braves to Milwaukee, the St. Louis Browns to Baltimore, the Philadelphia Athletics to Kansas City. These were clearly the efforts of moribund teams to survive. But in 1957 the removal of the tradition-rich Brooklyn Dodgers and New York Giants to, respectively, Los Angeles and San Francisco paved the way for the wholesale franchise movements that were to come later, and that in turn led to expansion, the establishment of teams all over the country.

So, for some baseball purists, the 1950s were "the last great decade." Eight teams in a league, as the game's "Founding Fathers" had so decreed. No divisional play, no league championship series, no artificial surfaces, no designated hitter, no free agency. For some it will seem like yesterday; for others, history, sweetened by time and mellowed by nostalgia.

Baseball in the '50s

Robin Roberts.

That's Jackie Robinson stealing third base against the Cardinals at Ebbets Field on July 26, 1950. Third baseman Tommy Glaviano and umpire Dusty Boggess are watching the play at second base, where Carl Furillo was stealing successfully on the back end of a double steal.

1·9·5·0

As the twentieth century creased in the middle and began the swing into its second half, New York City baseball was taking on a dynastic complexion. The Brooklyn Dodgers had won the pennant in 1947 and 1949 and were favorites to repeat in 1950, while the New York Yankees had also won in 1947 and 1949 and were similarly expected to win again in 1950. Well, when the final results were in, the prognosticators had scored one up and one down.

There were in the National League in 1950 two surprise teams, and one unsurprised manager. The surprise teams were the Dodgers, who did not win, and the Philadelphia Phillies, who did. The manager for whom it all worked out as expected was the Phillies' Eddie Sawyer.

"I don't know why anyone was surprised when we won," Sawyer said. "We had finished sixth in 1948 and then third in 1949, so we were on our way. We had good young ballplayers. Frankly, I would have been surprised if we *hadn't* won in 1950."

This was the Phillies team that came to be known, in deference to their relative youth, as "the Whiz Kids." The team included twenty-three-year-old Granny Hamner at shortstop, twenty-four-year-old Willie Jones at third, and twenty-five-year-old Del Ennis and twenty-three-year-old Richie Ashburn in the outfield; while the pitching staff was headed by right-hander Robin Roberts, twenty-three, and lefty Curt Simmons, twenty-one. Giving the team an even more unified aspect was the fact that they had all been developed in the Phillies' farm system. Mixed in with these striplings were veterans Eddie Waitkus at first base, Dick Sisler in the outfield, Andy Seminick behind the plate, and pitchers Russ Meyer and Jim Konstanty.

It was the thirty-three-year-old right-hander Konstanty, coming out of the bullpen 74 times, who made the difference. Throwing his palm-ball with uncanny efficiency all summer long, Big Jim (who was voted the National League's Most Valuable Player that year) won 16 and saved 22 (the save was not then a considered statistic; it has been computed retroactively). Roberts, one of the greatest of all National League pitchers, was 20–11, Simmons 17–8, young right-hander Bob Miller 11–6, and Meyer 9–11.

The Phillies' big gunner was Ennis, with 31 home runs, a .311 batting average, and a league-leading 126 runs batted in. Jones hit 25 homers and Seminick 24, while Ashburn batted .303.

In all probability, the Dodgers were the best team in the league that year. The boys from Brooklyn led the league in runs, hits, home runs, runs batted in, batting average, and slugging percentage. Brooklyn had Gil Hodges, Jackie Robinson, Pee Wee Reese, and Billy Cox in the infield, as good a defensive alignment as was ever seen on a major-league infield; Duke Snider and Carl Furillo the core of the outfield, and Roy Campanella catching (three more flawless glove men).

The Dodgers had three men with over 30 homers (Hodges 32 and Snider and Campanella 31 each) and three with over 100 runs batted in (Hodges 113, Snider 107, Furillo 106).

On the mound, the Brooks had a pair of 19-game winners in righty Don Newcombe and lefty Preacher Roe. The big difference between the two clubs lay in Philadelphia's league-leading 3.50 earned-run average, compared to Brooklyn's 4.24. The crucial difference was Konstanty, coming in all summer long to palm-ball late-inning rallies to death. The Dodgers had no comparable stopper in the pen.

The Dodgers scored 125 more runs than the Phillies, while the third-place Giants and the

1 · 9 · 5 · 0

fourth-place Braves also outscored the pennant winners, which reinforces a cherished baseball truism about pitching being 85 percent of the game.

The Braves had a 21-game winner in Warren Spahn, a 20-game winner in Johnny Sain, and a 19-gamer in Vern Bickford (who threw the league's only no-hitter, against the Dodgers in Boston on August 11). The Braves' staff delivered 88 complete games, a figure not bettered since in the league. The Boston staff thinned out considerably after their big three, however.

In the Department of No Surprises, the Cardinals' Stan Musial took his fourth batting title with a .346 average and Pittsburgh's Ralph Kiner was a gale in Pittsburgh's last-place doldrums, winning a fifth straight home run title with 47 big bangs. For individual explosions, the palm went to Gil Hodges, who hit four home runs against the Braves in Ebbets Field on August 31, while Musial put together a 30-game hitting streak from June 27 through July 26.

There was also an impressive streak that originated on the mound in 1950. The Giants' curve-balling right-hander Sal Maglie was four outs away from breaking Carl Hubbell's National League record of $46\frac{1}{3}$ consecutive scoreless innings. The streak was broken at the Polo Grounds when Pittsburgh's Gus Bell popped a 257-foot home run down the right-field line, two feet fair and just into the seats.

For the thirty-three-year-old Maglie, recently reinstated after having been suspended for jumping to the Mexican League in 1946, it was a surprisingly good year. Sal, who had developed a hard snap on his curve while pitching in the higher elevations of Mexico, turned in an 18–4 record.

In late July, the Phillies began pulling away from the Dodgers, Giants, and Braves, and by Labor Day had a seven-game lead. But then things began to happen to Sawyer's club; specifically, to their pitching staff. On September 10,

Simmons left for military duty. Miller was laid low by back problems. And on September 15, right-hander Bubba Church took a line drive in the face (the ball was hit by Ted Kluszewski, a notorious up-the-middle hitter).

Still, on September 19, the Whiz Kids were 7½ over Boston and 9 over Brooklyn. But then the shortage of arms began to tell. The Phillies dropped 8 of 11 while the Dodgers were taking 8 of 9.

By September 29, the Phillies were two in front of the Dodgers with two games remaining—both against the Brooks in Ebbets Field. The schedule makers couldn't have been more on the money.

The Dodgers took the first game, 7–3, behind right-hander Erv Palica. The Phillies were up against it now, a thoroughly dismayed club against a surging Dodger outfit. Sawyer sent out his ace, Robin Roberts, for the third time in five days, matching him against Brooklyn's big man, Don Newcombe. A Brooklyn win meant a tie and a three-game playoff, which would have been perilous for Sawyer's team—they were flat out of pitchers.

The two star right-handers matched each other in a tense pitching duel that went into the last of the ninth in a 1–1 tie. The first two Dodgers up, Cal Abrams and Pee Wee Reese, got on base. With Duke Snider at bat, Dodger manager Burt Shotton disdained the bunt and let the Duke swing away. Snider, who always raked Roberts fairly well, lashed a low, sizzling line drive to center field for a hit. If anything, Snider probably hit it too hard. With Abrams carrying the potential pennant-tying run around third, center fielder Richie Ashburn rushed in, picked up the ball, and fired home the most memorable peg of his life. Abrams was out by a good margin.

With Dodgers on second and third and only one out, Roberts was still standing on hot coals. Sawyer ordered the next batter, Jackie Robinson, walked ("A very good idea," Roberts said

1·9·5·0

later with a wry smile), filling the bases. However, neither of the next two hitters, Carl Furillo and Gil Hodges, was a bubble bath for a pitcher. But Roberts, reaching back for that seemingly bottomless strength that always amazed those who watched him pitch in a late-inning crisis, got Furillo to pop out and Hodges to fly out, and the gritty Phillies pitcher walked off the mound still tied.

In the top of the tenth inning the Phillies put two men on with none out. A sacrifice attempt resulted in a force play at third. The next batter was Dick Sisler, a big, strong, left-handed hitter. Newcombe pitched away from Sisler's power, but the big guy responded by hammering a high line drive that carried well back into the left-field stands for a three-run homer.

Roberts retired the Dodgers in order in the bottom of the tenth and the Phillies had their first pennant in 35 years, since 1915 and the glory days of Grover Cleveland Alexander.

The American League put on a spirited four-team race that was not decided until September 29, two days before the end of the season. When the last peanut shells had been swept from the grandstands, it was the New York Yankees up by three over Detroit, by four over Boston, and by six over Cleveland. As late as August 30, the four clubs had been separated by only two games.

For Casey Stengel's Yankees it was a second consecutive pennant. The Yankees, whose .282 team batting average was 20 points below Boston's .302, won their flag with a well-balanced squad that featured four .300 hitters (Joe DiMaggio, Hank Bauer, Yogi Berra, and MVP shortstop Phil Rizzuto, who had the greatest year of his career with a .324 batting average) and an exceptionally strong pitching staff. Stengel's starters were led by Vic Raschi (21–8), Eddie Lopat (18–8), Allie Reynolds (16–12), and Tommy Byrne (15–9). As if these four weren't enough, in mid-season the Yankees dipped into their perennially fertile farm system

and harvested another ripe yield in twenty-one-year-old left-hander Whitey Ford. This tow-headed product of New York's amateur baseball leagues, who in time was to become the greatest of all Yankee pitchers, broke in with nine consecutive victories and a 9–1 record overall.

For the thirty-five-year-old DiMaggio the shadows were growing longer. On August 11, the near unthinkable happened—Stengel had to bench his great star for weak hitting. Joe took a .279 batting average to the bench for a week, held his own counsel, and when he returned began ripping the ball in the style to which the customers had become accustomed. Joe finished at .301, with 32 home runs and 122 runs batted in.

Detroit's vigorous battle for the pennant (the Tigers won 95 games) was galvanized by third baseman George Kell's .340 batting average and league highs in hits (218) and doubles (56). Behind George was the .300-hitting outfield of Vic Wertz, Johnny Groth, and Hoot Evers. Skipper Red Rolfe's pitching was headed by right-handers Art Houtteman (19–12) and Fred Hutchinson (17–8). Detroit pitching suffered a heavy loss when right-hander Virgil Trucks was put out for the season with a sore arm in May.

The Red Sox had the league's most awesome batting attack, but they, too, were victimized by what was probably a pennant-costing injury. It occurred to super-slugger Ted Williams, who broke his elbow running down a fly ball in the All-Star Game in Comiskey Park. Williams got into just 89 games, batted .317, hit 28 home runs, and drove in 97 runs, better than an RBI per game.

With Williams out, Boston's heavy hitting was shared between rookie first baseman Walt Dropo, who batted .322, hit 34 homers, and tied for the league lead in runs batted in with teammate Vern Stephens with 144 apiece. (It was one of the most sensational rookie seasons of all time, but one which Dropo would never come

Joe DiMaggio.

Richie Ashburn, Phillies center fielder.

1·9·5·0

close to repeating.) Abetting the attack were second baseman Bobby Doerr, with a .294 batting mark, 27 homers, and 120 RBIs; third baseman Johnny Pesky, with a .312 batting average; outfielder Al Zarilla, .325; outfielder Dom DiMaggio, .328; catcher Birdie Tebbetts, .310; and shortstop Vern Stephens, .295, plus 30 home runs and those 144 runs batted in.

Perhaps Boston's most remarkable hitting was done by Billy Goodman, who singled and doubled his way to a league-leading .354 batting average despite a year-long status as utility player. Unable to find himself a regular spot on this slugging team, Goodman played 45 games in the outfield, 27 at third, 21 at first, and a handful at second. "That never bothered me," Billy said. "You have to remember what kind of ball club the Red Sox had in those years—an all-star at just about every position. I had a contract, and that's all that mattered."

So Boston finished third with the league's leading hitter having to scramble to get into a game. That meant the problem—as has been traditional in Boston—lay on the mound. The ace was southpaw Mel Parnell (18–10), followed by right-handers Joe Dobson and Ellis Kinder, both up in years and past their prime.

Give the Red Sox Cleveland's pitching in 1950 and the Fenway boys would have been unbeatable. To give some indication of the quality of Cleveland pitching that year, the Indians batted 33 points below the Bosox and finished just two games behind them in fourth place (winning 92 games, a hefty amount for a fourth-place club).

Cleveland player-manager Lou Boudreau had a staff of five right-handed starters: Bob Lemon (23–11), Early Wynn (18–8), Bob Feller (16–11), Mike Garcia (11–11), and Steve Gromek (10–7). Lemon's win total was the best in the league, and so was Wynn's 3.20 earned-run average.

The Indians had a few boppers in the lineup, three of whom knocked in over 100 runs—Luke Easter, Al Rosen, and Larry Doby—as well as a trio of .300 hitters in Doby, Dale Mitchell, and Ray Boone. This was a solid Cleveland club, but not enough to overcome the Boston firepower and the stronger balance in Detroit and New York. Rosen, with 37 home runs, became the first Cleveland player ever to lead the league in that department.

With the top four teams in the league playing such superior ball all season, there wasn't much for the second-division teams except a long hot summer. Finishing in the cellar were the Philadelphia Athletics, losers of 102 games, a windup that disappointed many of the game's sentimentalists. In 1949 the A's had finished fifth, but with a good-looking pitching staff, and there was some thought that they might contend in 1950. The prospect pleased a lot of people, who were thinking of the Athletics' owner and manager Connie Mack, baseball's grandfatherly image of kindness and eternity. The game's Methuselah was eighty-seven years old as the 1950 season began and still managing, though not with the same mental acuity and physical stamina as in years past. In his fiftieth season of managing his beloved Athletics, Connie was drifting in and out of senility with greater frequency. "I don't think he even knew my name," said Bobby Shantz, one of Connie's regular starters that year. Connie had been hanging on for "one more pennant," but it was not to be. After the season, the old gentleman retired, replaced by one of his former players, Jimmy Dykes, bringing to a close a big-league career that had begun in 1886.

The Rookies of the Year in 1950 both came from Boston—the Braves' outfielder Sam Jethroe in the National League and the Red Sox' Walt Dropo in the American.

The 1950 World Series wasn't really as lopsided as the final results made it look. Although the Yankees swept the Phillies in four, the scores gave a truer impression of a hard-fought series: 1–0, 2–1, 3–2, 5–2.

Stan Musial.

Stan Musial

He has been called the most amiable of all baseball's major stars. Musial's pleasant disposition made him one of the game's most widely admired and appreciated personalities. Once, when a newspaperman jokingly asked him why he was always smiling, Stan replied, "If you were me, wouldn't you be smiling?"

The smiles began on November 21, 1920, in Donora, Pennsylvania. Displaying his talents at an early age, Musial was signed into the St. Louis Cardinal organization as a pitcher in 1938. In 1940 Stan hurt his shoulder while racking up an 18–5 record for Daytona Beach in the Florida State League.

Normally, a sore shoulder for a young pitcher means a bus ride home and a lifetime of regret and wistful reminiscence. But this young southpaw could also swing the bat, rapping crackling line drives from a most singular stance, resembling, as someone said, "a kid peeking around the corner." It was all noticed by the Cardinals. Pitcher Musial became outfielder Musial.

In 1941 he started the season playing the outfield for the Springfield club in the West Virginia League. After 87 games young Stanley was batting .379. The Cardinals promoted him to Rochester, of the International League, where he batted .326 in 54 games, and then brought him to St. Louis for the final weeks of a sizzling pennant race with the Dodgers. Musial got into 12 games and under steamy pressure

batted .426. A lot of Cardinal players believed that if the club had brought Musial up a few weeks sooner they would have won the pennant.

Going into the 1950s, Musial was an established star, having already won three batting titles. He continued on as one of the National League's most lethal hitters, winning four more batting crowns, for a total of seven. In National League history, only Rogers Hornsby won as many, and only Honus Wagner won more (eight).

Musial's page in the record book looks like the sky on a clear summer night—filled with starry asterisks indicating which of his numbers were the league's best in a specific category in a specific year. In addition to those seven batting crowns, Musial also led in runs scored five times, hits six times, doubles eight times, triples five times, runs batted in twice, total bases six times, slugging percentage six times. He was voted the league's Most Valuable Player in 1943, 1946, and 1948.

At the time he retired, after the 1963 season, Musial held many of the most significant batting records in the National League, some of which were later broken by Henry Aaron and Pete Rose.

The outfield of the 1950 Yankee pennant winners. *Left to right:* Joe DiMaggio, Hank Bauer, Gene Woodling.

A trio of Boston Red Sockers whose bats boomed in 1950. *Left to right:* Ted Williams, Vern Stephens, Walt Dropo.

Johnny Sain, 20–13 in 1950.

George Kell, a .340 hitter for the Tigers in 1950.

Phil Rizzuto, the American League's MVP in 1950.

Vic Raschi, a 21-game winner for the Yankees in 1950.

Manager of the 1950 National League pennant winners, Eddie Sawyer.

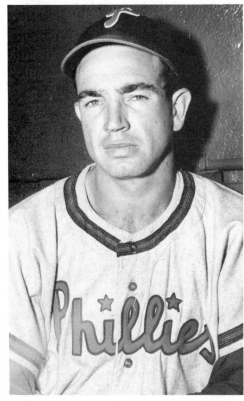

Willie Jones, Phillies third baseman.

Duke Snider.

Left to right: catcher Andy Seminick and outfielder Del Ennis of the Philadelphia Phillies.

Al Rosen, American League home-run champ in 1950.

Ralph Kiner, who hit 47 home runs in 1950.

Connie Mack.

Luke Appling. 1950 was the twentieth and last season for the great Chicago White Sox short-stop.

Jim Konstanty, Phillies relief ace and 1950's National League Most Valuable Player.

Marty Marion, the Cardinals' long-time shortstop.

Ted Williams.

Second baseman Bobby Doerr of the Red Sox. He drove in 120 runs in 1950, one year before a back injury forced him into premature retirement.

Walt Dropo—one of the greatest rookie seasons ever.

Red Sox outfielder Al Zarilla, one of seven .300 hitters on the 1950 Red Sox.

Joe Dobson, fine veteran right-hander of the Red Sox.

One of the hardest-hitting shortstops of all time: Vern Stephens of the Red Sox.

Pittsburgh left-hander Bill Werle.

The Yankees' slick double-play combination: Phil Rizzuto *(left)* and Jerry Coleman.

Right-hander Walter Masterson.

Dizzy Trout, veteran right-hander of the Detroit Tigers.

Howard Pollett of the Cardinals, one of the National League's classiest left-handers. He was 14–13 in 1950.

Sid Gordon, veteran New York Giants boomer who in 1950 was traded to the Boston Braves, for whom he hit 27 home runs and drove in 103 runs.

Cliff Fannin, St. Louis Browns right-hander.

Alvin Dark (left) and Eddie Stanky, the Giants' snappy keystone operators.

Catcher Joe Garagiola, who played for the Cardinals, Pirates, Cubs, and Giants in the 1950s.

Russ Meyer, the Phillies' colorful right-hander, known as "the Mad Monk."

Eddie Waitkus, the 1950 pennant winners' smooth-fielding first baseman.

Curt Simmons, fireballing left-hander of the Phillies.

Bob Miller, Phillies pitcher. He was 11–6 in 1950.

Granny Hamner, shortstop of "the Whiz Kids."

A trio of Boston Braves. *Left to right,* third baseman Bob Elliott, lefty Warren Spahn, outfielder Tommy Holmes. Elliott knocked in 107 runs in 1950, Spahn won his usual 21, and Holmes batted .298 while striking out just eight times in 105 games.

Outfielder Frank Baumholtz.

Cardinals pitcher George Munger.

Right-hander Cloyd Boyer, older brother of Ken and Clete.

Infielder Johnny Berardino, an 11-year major leaguer with the Browns, Indians, and Pirates. He later had a second, longer, and more prosperous career as one of the stars of TV's *General Hospital.*

Here's forty-three-year-old Luke Appling trying to steal third. The nifty hook slide didn't help, as Boston's Johnny Pesky has just slapped down the tag.

Brooklyn's Dan Bankhead, who in 1947 became the first black to pitch in the major leagues. In 1950, his only full season, he was 9–4.

Bud Podbielan, Dodger relief pitcher.

Third baseman Bob Dillinger of the Pirates, who obtained him from the Athletics in mid-season.

Vern Bickford, a 19-game winner for the Braves in 1950.

Erv Palica, hard-throwing Dodger righty who was 13–8 in 1950.

Detroit center fielder Johnny Groth, a .306 hitter in 1950.

Hoot Evers, who had a big year for the Tigers in 1950, batting .323 with 21 homers and 103 runs batted in.

Outfielder Jim Delsing, who moved around in the 1950s, playing for the Yankees, Browns, Tigers, and White Sox.

Cleveland ace Bob Lemon.

Lefty Bill Wight of the White Sox. They said he had the best pick-off move in the league.

Third baseman Hank Majeskie, a .309 hitter for the White Sox in 1950.

Catcher Birdie Tebbetts, who batted .310 in 1950.

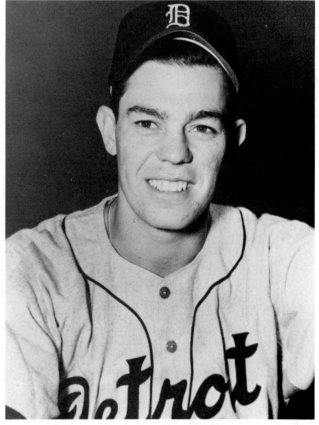

Right-hander Art Houtteman, Detroit's ace in 1950 with a 19–12 record.

Veteran left-hander Ken Heintzelman, who worked for the Phillies in 1950.

Phillies pitcher Bubba Church.

Outfielder Bill Nicholson, National League long-baller.

The Braves' Buddy Kerr, one of the league's finest fielding shortstops.

Detroit's Fred Hutchinson, a 17-game winner in 1950.

The Phillies' Dick Sisler, who hit the big one in the last game of the 1950 season.

Brooklyn's Cal Abrams, who never made it home in the last game.

Giants right-hander Sheldon Jones. They called him "Available" because he was always ready to pitch.

Dick Sisler getting the glad hand after his pennant-winning home run against the Dodgers.

Jim Konstanty at work against the Yankees in the fourth game of the 1950 World Series. Gene Woodling is the runner on first, Eddie Waitkus the first baseman.

Willie Mays.

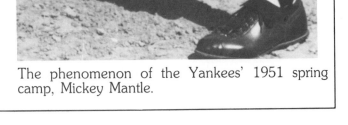

The phenomenon of the Yankees' 1951 spring camp, Mickey Mantle.

1·9·5·1

It was the year Joe DiMaggio retired, and it was the year Mickey Mantle and Willie Mays came to the major leagues as twenty-year-old rookies destined to become two of the greatest center fielders of all time. But it was an ex–center fielder who made the year his own with one swing of the bat, belting one of the game's most fabled and resounding home runs. His name was Bobby Thomson, his team the New York Giants, and he elevated what was an already highly charged moment into pure folklore.

The season that began so wretchedly for the Giants ended, on the afternoon of October 3, in air so thin it was the point where reality evaporates into fantasy. Selected by many experts to win the National League pennant in 1951, Leo Durocher's Giants hobbled out of the gate, losing 12 of their first 14, including 11 straight.

Charlie Dressen's Dodgers, meanwhile, went rolling through the league at flood tide and by August 11 had a 70–36 record and 13½-game lead over the Giants. Brooklyn had its usual stellar cast in place—with Roy Campanella, Gil Hodges, Jackie Robinson, Pee Wee Reese, Billy Cox, Duke Snider, Carl Furillo, and in a May 15 trade, Cub left fielder Andy Pafko, they had one of the strongest starting lineups in National League history. Indeed, the Brooks led the league in every offensive category except triples. Robinson topped the hitters with a .338 batting average, followed by Campanella's .325 (Roy was the Most Valuable Player that year), while Hodges hit 40 home runs, Campanella 33, and Snider 29.

On the mound, the Dodgers had southpaw Preacher Roe with a remarkable 22–3 record, followed by right-handers Don Newcombe (20–9), Carl Erskine, Ralph Branca, and Clyde King.

While the Dodgers were flying and the Giants kept rubbing the dust from their eyes, the rest of the league went about its business, and in cer-

tain quarters it was business as usual. In St. Louis Stan Musial took his fifth batting title with a .355 average, and in Pittsburgh Ralph Kiner won a sixth consecutive home run crown with 42 long ones.

Eddie Sawyer's Whiz Kids quickly earned themselves the unkind name "Fizz Kids" as they dropped to fifth place, which didn't stop Robin Roberts from winning 21. Boston's Warren Spahn won 22 (with 7 shutouts), while in Pittsburgh right-hander Murry Dickson won an eye-catching 20 games for a seventh-place club that won only 64 games all season (no other Pirate pitcher won more than 8), while Pittsburgh's left-hander Cliff Chambers pitched the league's only no-hitter, shutting down the Braves on May 6, 3–0.

The league's oddball event was certified in St. Louis's Sportsman's Park on the afternoon and evening of September 13. When the final meeting of the year between the Giants and Cardinals was rained out on September 12, the game was rescheduled for the following afternoon—with the Cardinals scheduled to play the Braves that night. The Cardinals ended up splitting the twin bill, beating the Giants in the afternoon and losing to the Braves at night. According to the records, it was the first such bit of byplay in the league since 1899.

On August 12, Durocher's Giants began to roll, putting on one of the most incredible stretch drives in baseball history. A solid club, the Giants had Wes Westrum catching, Whitey Lockman at first base, Eddie Stanky at second, Alvin Dark at short, and Bobby Thomson and Henry Thompson sharing third base. In the outfield were Monte Irvin (the RBI leader that year, with 121), Don Mueller, and the rookie who became the club's galvanizing force, Willie Mays. Mays was batting .477 at Minneapolis in the American Association when the floundering Giants reached down and brought him up in late May. The move sent center fielder Bobby

1·9·5·1

Thomson to third base. Willie's buoyant spirit and superb play both in the field and at bat began turning things around for the Giants. ("A kid that young, that good, and that spirited," said Irvin, "proved to be inspirational.") The youngster batted .274 and hit 20 home runs, in addition to setting new standards for center-field glovework. Willie was the league's Rookie of the Year.

Unable to match the Dodgers' batting power, the Giants had a cutting edge in the league's best pitching. The staff was headed by three right-handers: Sal Maglie (23–6), Larry Jansen (23–11), and Jim Hearn (17–9). Righty reliever George Spencer was 10–4, while veteran southpaw Dave Koslo was 10–9.

On August 12, the Giants began their dash to destiny by launching a 16-game winning streak (the league's best since 1935), during which they trimmed the Dodger lead to five games. Thereafter, whenever the Dodgers stubbed a toe it seemed the Giants were right behind them, gaining ground. By the end of the regular season, the Giants' surging trajectory had seen them take 37 of their last 44 games, earning them a flat-footed tie with the Dodgers for first place.

The Dodgers had been hard pressed in their last game to even come away with a dead heat. Going into extra innings against the Phillies in Philadelphia, Charlie Dressen's men were technically a half game behind, the Giants having won their game earlier. In the bottom of the twelfth, Jackie Robinson saved the game for the Dodgers with a sensational diving catch of a line drive with the bases loaded and two out; then, in the top of the fourteenth, Robinson won it for the beleaguered Dodgers with a home run. The stage was now set for a best-of-three pennant playoff with the Giants.

The Giants won the first game at Ebbets Field, 3–1, Hearn besting Branca. Game two, at the Polo Grounds, went to the Dodgers, 10–0,

rookie Clem Labine coasting behind Brooklyn's four-home-run attack.

The third game, also at the Polo Grounds, was the grand finale, the last and the biggest and the most pulsating of what seemed to have been four solid weeks of crucial and decisive games. Fittingly, each team had its ace on the mound, Newcombe for Brooklyn, Maglie for New York. Newk was 5–2 against the Giants that year, while Maglie was 5–1 against the Dodgers. Neither would figure in the decision.

With the game deadlocked at 1–1 going into the top of the eighth, the Dodgers put together a three-run rally on a walk and a series of singles, several of which skipped past third baseman Bobby Thomson, causing some grimacing on the Giants' bench.

Newcombe protected the lead through the bottom of the eighth. With Larry Jansen on the mound in the ninth, the Dodgers went quietly. Three more outs and the boys from Brooklyn would have put a last-minute cork in the Giants' bottle of miracles.

Only one of those outs was ever recorded.

This was Wednesday afternoon. On the previous Saturday, Newcombe had shut out the Phillies. On Sunday, he had come back to work 5⅔ shutout innings in the Dodgers' 14-inning cliff-hanger victory. Now here he was, pitching superb four-hit ball for 8 innings under the most extreme pressure. But the big, gallant right-hander couldn't get those last three outs.

Alvin Dark and Don Mueller opened with ground-ball singles into right field. Monte Irvin fouled out to Hodges. Whitey Lockman then dropped a double along the left-field line, scoring Dark and sending Mueller to third. (Mueller injured himself sliding into third, and a pinch runner, Clint Hartung, replaced him.) At this point, Dressen removed Newcombe and brought Ralph Branca in from the bullpen to face Bobby Thomson.

Branca threw a strike to Thomson, and then

1·9·5·1

another. It was this second one that Bobby turned into mythology when he lashed it on a line into the lower deck in left field, giving the Giants a sudden, startling, shocking 5–4 win and the pennant, sending Giant fans into contortions of ecstasy and leaving the usually garrulous Dodger fans silent with disbelief.

For the Dodgers and their fans, it was a compounding of bitter tastes: for the second year in a row, their club had fallen at the very end to a three-run homer (the Phillies' Dick Sisler having undone them the previous year); and worse, this time they had held a 13½-game lead in mid-August and allowed it to be dissipated; and just to heap humiliation upon ignominy, the loss was to the hated Giants.

For the Giants, this most theatrically achieved of all pennants was the club's first since 1937.

To match the throbbing drama of the National League pennant race, the American League could offer little, only a Yankee club that fought off a stubborn, pitching-rich Cleveland outfit in a march to a third straight pennant.

Casey Stengel still had the aging DiMaggio, though it was Joe's final year; and he also now had the nineteen-year-old rookie Mickey Mantle. The switch-hitting, power-hitting, winged-footed youngster from Oklahoma had stolen the headlines in the Yankee spring camp and, despite some misgivings on the part of the club's management, made the jump from Class C ball to the big leagues and opened the season in right field. Dogged by a mid-season slump, Mantle was optioned out for a month before returning and finishing up with 13 home runs and a .267 batting average. Despite this modest beginning, there was no doubt in the minds of all who saw him that the shy, quiet Oklahoman had the equipment to become one of the greatest of ballplayers.

Baseball, as we are often informed, is a serious business; but in 1951 there was a pixie

loose in it. His name was Bill Veeck and he owned the St. Louis Browns, one of the league's perennial tail-enders. Veeck possessed high good humor and an endearing sense of the absurd (essential qualities for an owner of the Browns to have). He also enjoyed sailing an occasional harpoon gently into the blubber of pomposity he saw around him. Throughout a long career in the game's executive suites, Veeck was responsible for many innovations, stunts, and zany promotions, all designed to make the game he loved more enjoyable. His masterpiece occurred during the 1951 season, in Sportsman's Park, St. Louis, on August 19.

In the last half of the first inning of the second game of a doubleheader against the White Sox, Browns manager Zack Taylor, at the behest of owner Veeck, sent up a pinch hitter for Frank Saucier. The pinch hitter was named Eddie Gaedel. It was Eddie's first major-league appearance. He was twenty-six years old, he was three feet, seven inches high, and wore number ⅛ on the back of his tiny uniform.

After Taylor showed the umpires a bona fide contract that Gaedel had signed, the game progressed—after White Sox pitcher Bob Cain was able to stop laughing. With Cain on the mound and Bob Swift catching, Gaedel (crouching, no less) walked on four pitches and then retired for a pinch runner.

Gaedel's big-league career was limited to that one appearance (though he has eternal life in baseball's trivia compilations), for American League president Will Harridge quickly gave the midget the boot, saying, "I feel that his participation in an American League championship game comes under the heading of conduct detrimental to baseball."

Stengel's Yankees won their pennant with a determined September surge, coming in five games ahead of Al Lopez's Indians, who had taken over first place for the last three weeks of August on the strength of a 44–19 record in

Two of the National League's more prolific muscle men, Gil Hodges *(left)* and Ralph Kiner. They had 82 home runs between them in 1951.

July and August. The Indians stumbled in September, however, and the Yankees didn't.

Cleveland lost despite having three 20-game winners—Bob Feller, Mike Garcia, and Early Wynn, plus Bob Lemon with 17. The Yankees, however, were able to match that with a pair of 20-gamers of their own in Eddie Lopat and Vic Raschi, and a 17-game winner in Allie Reynolds.

The hard-throwing Reynolds pitched a record-tying two no-hitters in 1951, the second of which ended on a note of high drama. Allie's first stifling came against Cleveland and Bob Feller on July 12, Reynolds winning 1–0 on Gene Woodling's home run. (Just 12 days before, on July 1, Feller had pitched the third no-hitter of his career, against Detroit.)

Reynolds's second no-hitter came against the Red Sox in the first game of a doubleheader at Yankee Stadium on September 28. With two out in the ninth and his masterpiece hanging in the balance, Reynolds was facing Ted Williams. Coming right at the greatest hitter in history with blazing fast balls, Allie got Williams to pop up behind the plate. Yankee catcher Yogi Berra drifted back, got under it—and dropped it, as nearly 40,000 Yankee fans groaned. The gutty Reynolds went back to the mound and fired another fast ball, and again Williams popped one up behind the plate. This time Berra—with an anxiety-ridden Reynolds at his side—caught it. The win clinched a tie for the pennant for the Yankees (they took it all in the second game behind Raschi) and made Reynolds only the second pitcher in baseball history to deliver two no-hitters in a season, the other being Johnny Vander Meer and his two consecutive gems in 1938.

The Yankees won the pennant with only Rookie of the Year infielder Gil McDougald batting over .300 (.306). In his final year, DiMaggio batted .263, while the star of the team was Berra with 27 home runs, 88 runs batted in, and a .294 batting average.

The American League home run champ that year was the big, right-handed-hitting Gus Zernial, who opened the season with the White Sox but was soon traded to the Athletics, for whom he hit all of his 33 home runs. Zernial was also the RBI leader, with 129. In addition,

the sixth-place Athletics also had the league's leading batter in first baseman Ferris Fain, who surprised everyone by batting .344, giving the club a Triple Crown of sorts.

Between them, the Yankees and the Indians had five of the league's six 20-game winners, and it was the sixth who may have had the most remarkable season of all. He was right-hander Ned Garver of the last-place (102 losses) St. Louis Browns. Pitching for what was probably baseball's most inept team, Garver managed to win 20 and lose 12, completing 24 of his 30 starts. No other Browns pitcher won more than six.

On July 12 and 13, right after the All-Star break, the Red Sox and White Sox put in a couple of nights' work that proved to be monumental. On the twelfth, the two clubs played a twi-night doubleheader. Boston won the first game, 3–2, in nine innings, and the nine innings are stressed because the second game went 17 innings before Boston won it 5–4. Reliever Ellis Kinder pitched 10 scoreless innings. Right-hander Saul Rogovin went the full 17 for Chicago. The next night the clubs went at it again, this time for 19 innings, before the White Sox won 5–4. Lefty Mickey McDermott went the first 17 innings for Boston, while the White Sox used three pitchers.

In the World Series, the Giants extended the Yankees to six games before running out of miracles. Thomson's home run had made the Series seem anticlimactic, and the losers took it in stride. "When Thomson hit that home run," Monte Irvin said later, "that was our season, right there. The rest was gravy."

Speaking of gravy, it might be interesting to quote from a report that included major-league salaries in that 1951 season. The entire American League payroll was approximately $2,750,000, with the Yankees carrying the highest burden at just under $500,000. The National League payroll was around $2,500,000, with the Cardinals leading with $385,000. The average big-league salary was about $12,500. The minimum salary at that time was $5,000, climbing all the way up to the $90,000 reportedly being paid DiMaggio and Williams.

Yogi Berra.

Yogi Berra

Slowly, year by year, Yogi Berra built his reputation as one of baseball's most lethal clutch hitters and one of its canniest catchers. Among certain segments of sportswriters and fans, Berra was more celebrated for his malapropism (many of which he never uttered), but within the circles of baseball people, he was always taken seriously. "My assistant manager, Mr. Berra" was how Casey Stengel often referred to him. "Listen to what he says, not how he says it," said Gil Hodges, Mets manager, for whom Berra coached.

They called him a "bad-ball hitter," meaning that he swung at anything and everything. But some pitchers maintained that this was not precisely so; they said Yogi was a guess hitter, and that when he guessed correctly he swung at the ball no matter where it was. But when a game was on the line in the late innings, said Warren Spahn (who pitched to Yogi in a couple of World Series), Berra became the most fastidious of hitters and would not swing at a ball if it was an inch or two off the plate.

Berra was born in St. Louis on May 12, 1925. Somehow, the Cardinals, who soaked up young talent like a sponge, overlooked him. The Yankees signed him in 1943 and sent him to Norfolk in the Piedmont League, where Yogi (he was known as Larry then—Lawrence Peter Berra) caught for one year before going into the Navy. Upon being discharged in 1946, he played for the top Yankee farm club at Newark in the International League. He batted .314 and came up to the big club for a look-see at the end of the season. He batted .364 in seven games and was up to stay.

By the beginning of the 1950s, Berra was a star among stars, along with Joe DiMaggio and Phil Rizzuto one of the centerpoles of a juggernaut Yankee team.

From 1950 through 1959, the Yankees had six of the league's ten Most Valuable Players, and three times it was Berra—in 1951, 1954, and 1955.

When Yogi was breaking in in 1947, his tutor was the recently retired Yankee catching great Bill Dickey. "Dickey is teaching me his experience," Yogi said in a memorable quote. The pupil learned well. Known primarily for his hitting, Berra gradually developed into a superb defensive catcher. From July 28, 1957, through May 10, 1959, Berra caught 148 consecutive games without an error, during which he handled 950 chances, both major-league records for a catcher.

He was a power hitter—358 lifetime home runs—with a pair of the sharpest of batting eyes, never striking out more than 38 times in a season.

Getting into 14 World Series, Berra holds numerous records for postseason play, including most Series, most games (75), most at bats (259), most hits (71); and on October 2, 1947, he became the first man to pinch-hit a home run in a World Series.

Sal Maglie, 23–6 in 1951.

Bobby Thomson.

Larry Jansen, 23–11 in 1951.

Casey Stengel.

Twilight and sunrise: DiMaggio and Mantle in 1951.

Eddie Gaedel in his debut and farewell performance. The catcher is Bob Swift. The pitch is definitely high.

Stan Musial scored 1,949 runs in his career. This is one of them.

Gil McDougald, who batted .306 in his rookie year.

Tom Morgan. The Yankee rookie was 9–3 in his first year.

Billy Goodman, the American League's 1950 batting champion, receiving his emblematic silver bat from league president Will Harridge in May 1951.

Murry Dickson, a 20-game winner for the seventh-place Pirates in 1951.

Lou Boudreau, Cleveland's great shortstop of the 1940s, who wound up his playing career with the Red Sox in the early 1950s.

Ned Garver, who was 20–12 for the last-place St. Louis Browns in 1951.

Robin Roberts warming up in the left-field bullpen at the Polo Grounds.

Bob Feller, 22–8 in 1951, the last of his six 20-game seasons.

Bob Feller at work on the mound at Yankee Stadium. Al Rosen is the third baseman.

Brooklyn's Don Newcombe, 20–9 in 1951.

Preacher Roe, Brooklyn's cagey south-paw, who posted a scintillating 22–3 in 1951.

Dodger right-hander Clyde King, 14–7 in 1951.

Eddie Miksis. This versatile utility man played for the Dodgers, Cubs, Cardinals, Orioles, and Reds in the 1950s.

Three Boston Red Sox southpaws gather together for the cameraman. *Left to right:* Chuck Stobbs, Mel Parnell, Mickey McDermott.

Ray Scarborough, 12–9 for the Red Sox in 1951.

Dominic DiMaggio, superb center fielder of the Boston Red Sox.

Red Sox shortstop Johnny Pesky, a .313 hitter in 1951.

Clyde Vollmer of the Boston Red Sox, a journeyman outfielder who astonished everyone in the month of July, when he hit 13 home runs and drove in 40 runs, doing most of that hitting in clutch situations.

Dominic's big brother.

Eddie Lopat. They called this Yankee southpaw "Steady Eddie." In 1951 he was 21–9. *(Photo by Bob Olen.)*

Bobby Brown, the Yankees' line-drive-hitting third baseman, who later became president of the American League.

Cardinals outfielder Peanuts Lowrey, a .303 hitter in 1951.

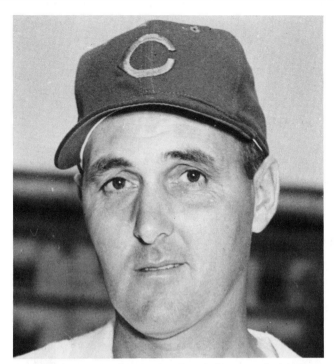

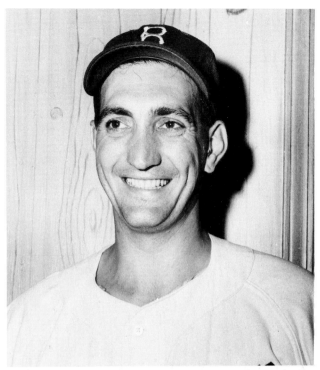

The veteran knuckle baller Dutch Leonard. Ageless, like most knuckle ballers, the forty-two-year-old Leonard was the kingpin of the Cubs' bullpen in 1951 with a 10–6 record.

Ralph Branca. He wasn't superstitious, because he wore number 13. In 1951 he won 13 games and pitched 13 complete games. And then *It* happened.

It's July 2, 1951, and Bob Feller *(center)* has just pitched his third career no-hitter, against Detroit. Sharing the smiles of the moment are Sam Chapman *(left)* and Luke Easter. Chapman and Easter produced the hits that provided Feller with his winning margin.

St. Louis Browns first baseman Hank Arft.

Ray Coleman, outfielder with the Browns and White Sox in 1951. Ray was batting .282 when the Browns, apparently embarrassed by a respectable batting average, traded him.

Leo Durocher *(left)* and three of his "miracle" Giants. *Left to right:* Willie Mays, Monte Irvin, and Henry Thompson.

Some New York Giant timbermen. *Left to right:* Bobby Thomson, Don Mueller, Monte Irvin, White Lockman.

That's a nice fall-away slide Willie Mays is putting on, but he's clearly going to be out as Roy Campanella applies the tag. Al Barlick is the umpire. It happened at the Polo Grounds on September 2, 1951.

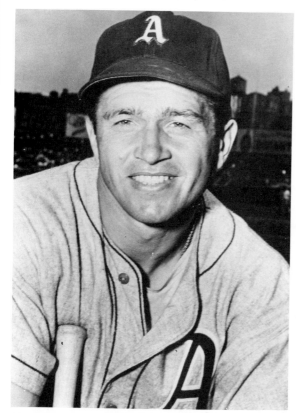

Elmer Valo, Philadelphia Athletics outfielder, who batted .302 in 1951.

Cleveland outfielder Sam Chapman.

Minnie Minoso, the Chicago White Sox' popular and talented outfielder. He batted .324 in 1951.

Boston Braves outfielder Willard Marshall.

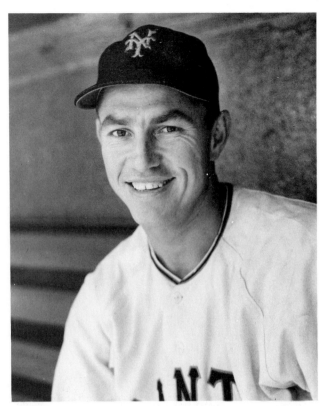

Monte Kennedy, the New York Giants' hard-throwing but erratic left-hander.

Left-hander Dave Koslo of the New York Giants.

Veteran National Leaguer Johnny Hopp, who joined the Yankees late in the season and helped them to the pennant.

Sam Jethroe, speedy outfielder of the Boston Braves, who led the National League in steals in 1951, with 35.

The seasoned left-hander of the St. Louis Cardinals, Max Lanier.

Bob Swift, Detroit's veteran catcher.

Allie Reynolds: 17–8 in 1951, including two no-hitters.

A bit of action early in the third game of the Dodger-Giant pennant playoff at the Polo Grounds. Sal Maglie has attempted a sacrifice bunt, but Don Newcombe picked it up and is firing to second base (being covered by Pee Wee Reese) to force Wes Westrum.

Branca has pitched and Thomson has swung and the confetti is beginning to fall as Dodger left fielder Andy Pafko stands helplessly at the base of the wall.

Bobby Thomson coming home.

Starting pitchers for Game 2 of the 1951 World Series: Larry Jansen of the Giants *(left)* and the Yankees' Eddie Lopat.

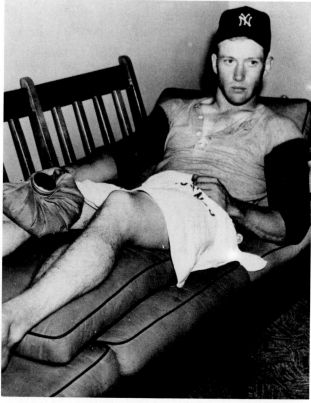

For Mickey Mantle it was to be a career plagued by injuries. The first serious one occurred in the second game of the 1951 World Series when he hurt his knee while chasing a fly ball.

Brooklyn relief pitcher Joe Black, the key man in the club's drive to the 1952 pennant.

1·9·5·2

Baseball people wondered what effect Brooklyn's crushing and heartbreaking last-minute loss in 1951 would have on the club in 1952. Complicating things for Charlie Dressen's team was the loss of ace right-hander Don Newcombe to military service for two years.

The Dodgers, however, still had the most potent lineup in the league: Hodges, Robinson, Reese, and Cox in the infield; Furillo, Snider, and Pafko in the outfield; and Campanella catching.

On the mound, the Dodgers received unexpected and sensational service from twenty-eight-year-old rookie right-hander Joe Black, a big, strong, hard thrower who wasn't even on the roster in spring training. Working out of the bullpen all year, Black was 15–4 with 15 saves, earning himself Rookie of the Year honors. Carl Erskine, with a 14–6 record, was the club's next-highest winner.

Leo Durocher's Giants jumped off to a fast start, winning 26 of their first 34, and were in first place until the end of May—significantly, until Willie Mays was called into the Army for two years. That, combined with the loss of the team's big RBI man Monte Irvin, caused the erosion of the 1952 Giants. Irvin had broken his ankle sliding into third base in an exhibition game in Denver in early April, and didn't return until late in the season. By that time, the Dodgers had built a 10½-game lead.

The Giants, despite the back ailments that afflicted ace right-handers Maglie and Jansen, did make a late-season charge at the Dodgers that was menacing enough to evoke nightmares of 1951. The Giants were aided immensely by a twenty-eight-year-old relief pitching rookie of their own, Hoyt Wilhelm, master of a tantalizing knuckle ball that was going to provide major-league employment for him for twenty years. Wilhelm worked in a league-high 71 games, posting a 15–3 record with 11 saves and the league's lowest ERA, 2.43.

By September 14, the Giants had trimmed their first-place deficit to 3 games, but this time the Dodgers held firm (thanks largely to the stalwart Black) and won by 4½. Brooklyn's pennant in 1952 was won primarily because of a crushing supremacy they maintained over the three bottom clubs, Cincinnati, Boston, and Pittsburgh, whom they devoured with a 54–11 record.

Overall, it was not an outstanding year for National League pitchers. There was only one 20-game winner, no 19-game winner, and just one 18-game winner (Maglie). That 20-game winner, however, turned in one of the finest sustained pitching performances of modern times. Robin Roberts of the Philadelphia Phillies not only clocked his third straight season of 20 or more victories, but this time climbed all the way to 28–7, running up the highest win total in the league since Dizzy Dean had won that many for the Cardinals in 1935.

Roberts completed 30 of 37 starts, pitched 330 innings, and walked just 45.

While Roberts was working through a season of almost unbroken success, Stan Musial continued his own high-caliber consistency, winning his third straight batting title and sixth overall with a .336 batting average.

Home run honors were divided between Chicago's Hank Sauer and Pittsburgh's Ralph Kiner, each with 37 when the final bell rang. For Kiner it was a seventh straight home run title (it was the third time he had tied for it), something that not even Babe Ruth had ever done. Ralph's big bat, along with talented rookie shortstop Dick Groat, was about all the Pirates had in a dismal 1952 season, during which they lost 112 games. Murry Dickson, 1951's 20-game winner, was 14–21, which was something akin to heroic on that club; Murry won exactly a third of his team's games.

For Hank Sauer it was a banner year. Along with his 37 home runs, the Cubs' slugger drove

1·9·5·2

in 127 runs, good enough to lead the league and earn him the Most Valuable Player award. Sauer's MVP designation stirred some controversy; there were those who thought it should have more properly gone to one of three pitchers—Black, Wilhelm, or Roberts.

For single-inning outbursts, there was nothing to compare with what happened in the bottom of the first inning at Ebbets Field on the night of May 21. After retiring the Cincinnati Reds quietly in the top of the inning, the Dodgers spent the better part of the next two hours circling the bases and dispatching Cincinnati pitchers. By the time that first inning was completed, the Dodgers had scored 15 runs (a National League record since 1900), on their way to an eventual 19–2 victory.

That first inning went on for so long that the Reds' starting pitcher, Ewell Blackwell, quickly kayoed, took a shower, dressed, and hailed a cab back to his Manhattan hotel. He walked into the lounge, took a seat at the bar, morosely glanced up at the television set, and asked the bartender what inning it was.

"Bottom of the first," the bartender said.

A few moments later, Bud Byerly, Blackwell's relief pitcher, walked in, also freshly showered. He sat down next to Blackwell and asked what inning it was.

"Bottom of the first," Blackwell said.

Byerly didn't say anything.

"Don't you want to know what the score is?" Blackwell asked.

"Frankly," Byerly said, "no."

The other side of this fiasco was the near perfection of Brooklyn's Carl Erskine on June 19 at Ebbets Field. The classy, curve-balling Dodger right-hander no-hit the Cubs, his performance marred only by the base on balls he issued in the third inning to the Chicago starter Willard Ramsdell.

Coming into the National League that season was a husky twenty-year-old third baseman with the Boston Braves, Eddie Mathews. Eddie batted just .242 but hit 25 home runs, showing evidence of the power that would account for 512 homers before his career was over.

In the American League, Casey Stengel's Yankees marched to the beat of their own drummer for the fourth year in a row, tying a major-league record by making it 4-for-4 for the Old Man.

With Mickey Mantle in center field now in place of the retired DiMaggio, the Yankees fought a summers-long battle against a determined Cleveland Indians club. Complicating the Yankees' struggle was the loss to the military of infielders Bobby Brown and Jerry Coleman and pitcher Tom Morgan (Whitey Ford was spending his second year in the service).

Stengel's patchwork infield was still a good one, with Joe Collins at first, Billy Martin at second, the veteran Phil Rizzuto at short, and the versatile Gil McDougald at third. Along with Mantle, who led the club with a .311 batting average, the outfield consisted of Gene Woodling (.309) and Hank Bauer (.293), a couple of solid performers.

The Yankee pitching still featured Allie Reynolds (20–8 and leading in shutouts, strikeouts, and earned-run average), Vic Raschi, Eddie Lopat, and National League pickup Johnny Sain, who started and relieved with equal success.

Al Lopez's Indians again were powerful on the mound, with three 20-game winners—Early Wynn (23–12), Bob Lemon, and Mike Garcia (each at 22–11). Bob Feller, his once-mighty fast ball beginning to fade, disappointed with a 9–13 record.

Offensively, the Indians were a match for the Yankees, with Larry Doby leading the league with 32 home runs, Luke Easter right behind him with 31, and Al Rosen with 28. Rosen was the league's runs-batted-in leader with 105, one

1·9·5·2

more than Doby and Chicago's Eddie Robinson. It was the lowest total for an American League RBI leader since 1918.

The Indians got away quickly when the season opened, while the Yankees progressed more deliberately. Lopez's team held on to first place until June 9, when they relinquished it to the Yankees, who maintained occupancy for the rest of the season, except for a day in June and another in August.

Both clubs played torrid ball in September—they had identical 19–5 records—and the Indians pulled to within half a game of the lead on September 12, but at the end the Yankees had their pennant by a two-game margin.

With a war blazing in Korea, a number of big leaguers were called to military service, most prominent among them Boston's Ted Williams. As a member of the Marine Air Corps Reserves, Ted was subjected to recall, and recalled he was, at the end of April. After having put in three years during World War II, Williams was understandably unhappy at having a second large dent put in his career, and he let a few people know about it. But off he went, flying some hair-raising combat missions in Korea before returning late in the 1953 season.

The league's outstanding pitcher in 1952, and ultimately its Most Valuable Player, was the Athletics' five-foot-six-inch left-hander Bobby Shantz. With a curve ball that broke almost as wide as he was tall, Shantz was dynamite all season, posting a 24–7 record and completing 27 of his 33 starts. Bobby's mound partner, right-hander Harry Byrd, broke in at 15–15 and was voted the American League's Rookie of the Year. Giving the fourth-place A's further honors was first baseman Ferris Fain, whose .327 batting average gave him his second batting crown in a row. With Musial winning again in the National League, it marked the first time since 1914 that both batting champions repeated.

There was also another repeat performance of note. When Allie Reynolds fired two no-hitters in 1951, it was a first in the American League. Well, in 1952, Detroit's fast-balling right-hander Virgil Trucks matched Reynolds. On May 15 at Detroit, Trucks no-hit the Washington Senators, winning 1–0 when Vic Wertz blasted a home run with two out in the bottom of the ninth. On August 25, Trucks stunned the Yankees in New York with another no-hitter, again winning by a 1–0 score, retiring the last 20 batters in a row.

What made Truck's performances particularly eye-catching was his season's record: 5–19. Of course, he was working for an eighth-place club, and this was also worth some passing historical notice, for it was the first time since they entered the American League in 1901 that a Detroit team had finished last.

The Tigers had another flash of glory in addition to Trucks' no-hitters. First baseman Walt Dropo, obtained from the Red Sox in a June trade, muscled his way into the record books by getting 12 consecutive hits over three games, on July 14 and a July 15 doubleheader. Big Walter's hot streak equaled the major-league record set by Pinky Higgins in 1938.

For Boston Red Sox fans it was a September of worst dreams come true. Chided by their critics for late-season folds, Fenway fans saw their heroes outdo themselves that year. Just 5½ games off the pace at the end of August, and nurturing hopes, the Red Sox went flat in September with a 7–20 record and ended in sixth place, 19 games out. The dismal overall picture included a 26–51 road record.

In the World Series, the Yankees outlasted the Dodgers, four games to three, despite Duke Snider's four home runs, which tied a Series record held by Babe Ruth and Lou Gehrig.

Robin Roberts.

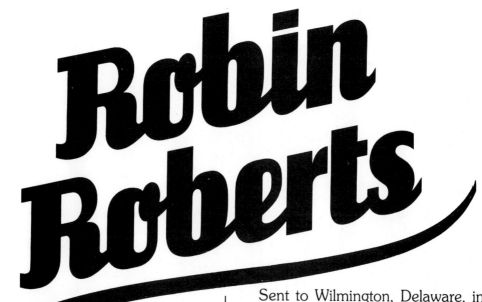

Robin Roberts

When asked about his ace pitcher, Phillies manager Eddie Sawyer said, "Robin Roberts? One of the greatest pitchers of all time. If we'd had a little better ball club, with one or two more hitters, he probably could have won 400 games. He was a pleasure for any manager to have on his ball club. He was difficult to handle for only one reason—he wanted to pitch every day and thought he could. He completed many games with only 70 or 75 pitches, so there were times when I didn't think twice about letting him go out there with only two days' rest.

"He did it with speed, control, and stamina. He seldom threw a ball above the belt, and most of the time he was right across the knees with it. And he had the ability to draw back and throw a little bit harder when he had to. He had a very easy delivery. I call it symmetry of motion. It just flowed, pitch after pitch. He made it look easy."

Roberts was born in Springfield, Illinois, on September 30, 1926. He was a fine all-around athlete, but baseball was the game closest to his heart. He first attracted attention pitching for Michigan State and then for a semipro league in Vermont in 1947.

The Phillies brought him to Wrigley Field in Chicago for a tryout in the fall of 1947. After watching him throw, one of the Phillie coaches said, "Don't let that kid get away." They didn't. Roberts signed for a $20,000 bonus.

Sent to Wilmington, Delaware, in the Interstate League, Roberts pitched in just 11 games, rang up a 9–1 record, and was promptly brought up by the Phillies. After going 7–9 and 15–15 in his first two seasons, he began in 1950 a string of six straight 20-game seasons, the first National League pitcher since Christy Mathewson to achieve success of that kind.

"Speed, control, and stamina," said Eddie Sawyer, and this was what Roberts demonstrated throughout the heyday of his glittering career. Content to let batters hit the ball, he led in strikeouts only twice. "He never tried to strike you out," an opponent said, "unless he had to. Then he usually did. I think if you went back through the records, you'd see he got a lot of his whiffs with a man on third and less than two out."

Though working over 300 innings for six straight years, Roberts never walked more than 77 batters in a season, and in fact went over 70 walks only twice in his 19-year career.

For five straight years (1952–1956) Roberts led the National League in complete games, a span during which he completed 140 of 191 starts.

When it was all over, Roberts had a lifetime record of 286–245. Did he regret not getting those last 14 victories?

"Well, 300 would have been nice," he said. "But I don't have any regrets. When it was all over, I went home smiling."

Giants reliever Hoyt Wilhelm, who began a 21-year career with a brilliant rookie season in 1952.

Cubs outfielder Hank Sauer, the National League's Most Valuable Player in 1952.

Jackie Robinson.

Brooklyn shortstop Pee Wee Reese, the National League's leading base stealer in 1952, with 30.

Brooklyn left fielder Andy Pafko.

Gil Hodges.

Outside Detroit's Briggs Stadium.

Virgil Trucks gives the "double-zero" sign after pitching his second no-hitter of the year against the Yankees on August 25.

Yankee first baseman Joe Collins. He hit 18 homers in 1952.

The Philadelphia Athletics' Bobby Shantz, whose 24–7 record earned him American League MVP honors.

Big John Mize, Casey Stengel's pinch hitter deluxe.

Yankee second baseman Billy Martin. He was called "scrappy" then, and a lot of other things since.

Mr. Musial at bat. Roy Campanella is the catcher.

Cincinnati's Ewell Blackwell. His sidearm delivery was a nightmare for right-handed batters.

Ken Raffensberger, Cincinnati's veteran southpaw, who was 17–13 in 1952.

Cincinnati third baseman Bobby Adams.

Grady Hatton, who played second and third for the Reds in the early 1950s.

Lefty Al Brazle. He won 12 and saved 16 coming out of the bullpen for the Cardinals in 1952.

Harry Brecheen, the crafty "Cat" of the Cardinals' mound corps.

Brooklyn's Billy Cox stealing home on the front end of a double steal against the Cardinals at Ebbets Field on May 13, 1952. Del Rice is the catcher. Umpire Art Gore is flashing the safe sign.

Del Rice, Cardinals catcher through the first half of the 1950s.

Gil Coan, Washington Senators outfielder.

Washington shortstop Pete Runnels, a .285 hitter in 1952.

Two-time American League batting champion Ferris Fain of the Philadelphia Athletics.

Safe at third is Boston's Dom DiMaggio.

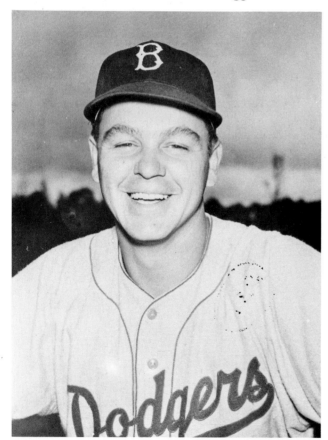

Dick Williams, Brooklyn utility man in 1952, who later became a highly successful manager.

Brooklyn outfielder George Shuba, who batted .305 in 1952.

Al Corwin, Giants reliever in 1952, who was 6–1.

Johnny Rutherford, Dodger right-hander in 1952.

Chicago Cubs player-manager Phil Cavaretta.

Bob Rush, ace righty of the Chicago Cubs. He was 17–13 in 1952.

The Athletics' Bobby Shantz dropping a sacrifice bunt against the Washington Senators at Griffith Stadium. The catcher is Clyde Kluttz, the umpire Ed Rommel. The action took place on August 10.

Cleveland first baseman Luke Easter. He had 31 homers in 1952.

Cardinals right-hander Stu Miller. He baffled hitters with three pitches: slow, slower, and slowest.

Joe Presko, Cardinals pitcher.

Satchel Paige, the ageless wonder. Forty-five years old in 1952, he was 12–10 for the Browns.

Philadelphia Athletics shortstop Eddie Joost. He had 20 homers in 1952.

Dale Mitchell, a man with a .300-caliber bat. The Cleveland outfielder batted .323 in 1952.

Paul Minner, Chicago Cubs southpaw, who was 14–9 in 1952.

White Sox right-hander Saul Rogovin, 14–9 in 1952.

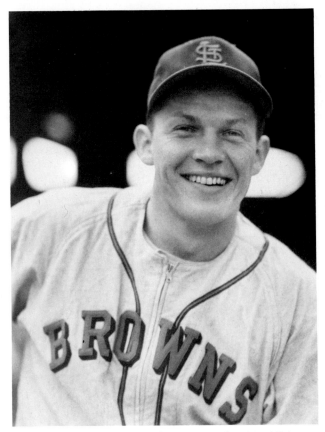

Browns outfielder Bob Nieman, who hit 18 home runs in 1952.

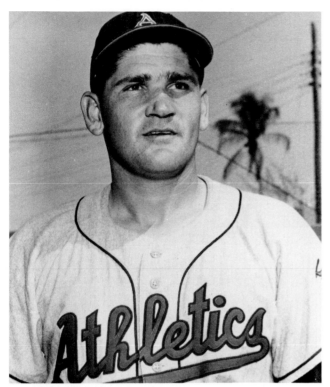

Alex Kellner, the Athletics' big left-hander.

Left-hander Bill Henry, Red Sox relief pitcher.

Steve Gromek, Cleveland's fifth starter, after Wynn, Lemon, Garcia, and Feller.

Cubs first baseman Dee Fondy, a .300 hitter in 1952.

Johnny Antonelli. The Braves signed him for a large bonus in 1948, then traded him to the Giants in 1954, just as he was about to become one of the league's premier pitchers.

1·9·5·3

For 52 years Boston had been a two-team town, with local loyalties divided between the Red Sox and Braves. That division had never been truly equitable, however; Boston was known as a "Red Sox town." The gulf between the two clubs was never more evident than in 1952, when the Sox drew over 1,100,000 customers and the Braves a mere 281,000.

So, in the spring of 1953, the Braves applied for and received permission to move their franchise to Milwaukee. It marked the first break in the alignment of either major league since 1902, and it was the beginning of a rearrangement of the big leagues that would see teams migrate around the country. What made the subsequent moves inevitable was the financial success of the Braves in Milwaukee; it was immediate and astounding. The Braves' attendance rocketed from 281,000 in 1952 to 1,826,000 in 1953, then cleared the two million mark for the next four years.

The move also seemed to effect a spiritual rejuvenation as well—the Braves surged from seventh place to second.

Second place was gratifying for the Braves, but they needed a pair of field glasses to see first place that year. Repeating as pennant winners were Charlie Dressen's Brooklyn Dodgers, fielding what many people still regard as one of the greatest teams in National League history. The Dodgers took over first place at the end of June and thereafter proceeded to massage the league and dispel any notions of a pennant race. From the All-Star break to September 1, Dressen's boys took 41 of 50 games and clinched the pennant on September 12, the earliest clinching date in National League history.

The Dodgers combined for a .285 team batting average and hit 208 home runs, second in major-league history only to the 1947 Giants' 221. From June 18 through July 10, the Dodgers homered in 24 consecutive games, breaking the league record of 19 set by the 1947 Giants and falling one short of the 1941 Yankees' major-league standard.

Duke Snider rapped 42 and Roy Campanella 41 homers, making the Dodgers the first National League club ever to have two players with 40 home runs in a single year. Five Dodgers hit over .300: Carl Furillo, .344; Snider, .336; Jackie Robinson, .329; Campanella, .312; and Gil Hodges, .302. Billy Cox batted .291, Pee Wee Reese .271, and Rookie of the Year second baseman Jim Gilliam .278. Campanella, who drove in 142 runs to lead the league, was voted Most Valuable Player for the second time.

There was a story behind Furillo's batting championship. In a game against the Giants at the Polo Grounds on September 6, Furillo was hit by a pitch thrown by right-hander Ruben Gomez. Standing on first base, the hot-tempered Furillo began an irate exchange of words with Giant skipper Leo Durocher, whom Furillo suspected had ordered the errant pitch, and who was not one of Carl's favorite people anyway. The steamy words led to a challenge that led to a brawl as the two men charged each other (each man was most capable of defending his point of view). When the last epithet had floated skyward, Furillo had a broken hand (from being stepped on and not, as Carl would have preferred, from coming in contact with Leo's manly features) and a batting average frozen at .344. The .344 withstood the assaults of a pair of Cardinals—Red Schoendienst and Stan Musial—neither of whom could bring down the stationary target, Red finishing at .342 and Stanley at .337.

The Brooklyn ace that year was Carl Erskine with a 20–6 record, followed by double-digit winners Russ Meyer, Billy Loes, Preacher Roe, and relief ace Clem Labine. Overall, the Dodgers won 105 games, not to be exceeded in the National League until Cincinnati's 108 wins in

1·9·5·3

1975 (in a 162-game schedule).

The league's best pitching in 1953 belonged to the transplanted Braves, led by 23-game winner Warren Spahn. Behind the great lefty were right-handers Lew Burdette and Bob Buhl, and a gifted young southpaw named Johnny Antonelli, whom the Braves would misguidedly trade to the Giants in 1954.

The biggest surprise in the league in 1953, and the biggest crowd pleaser for Milwaukee's exuberant new fans, was sophomore third baseman Eddie Mathews. The twenty-one-year-old muscleman hit 47 home runs, leading the league and ending Ralph Kiner's seven-year reign as National League home run king. Kiner, in a startling mid-season trade, had been dealt to the Cubs as the pivotal man in a multiplayer swap. Kiner's combined Pirates-Cubs home run total was 35, placing him fifth behind Mathews, Campanella, Snider, and Cincinnati's muscular first baseman Ted Kluszewski, who poled 40 homers.

The year before, Kluszewski had hit just 16 homers. What accounted for this sudden surge? Big Klu explained: "In spite of my size, when I came up I was a spray hitter. It was the pitchers who forced me into hitting home runs. They found out they couldn't pitch me outside because I'd go with the ball. So they started coming inside. Well, if you adjust correctly you have to pull the ball, and when you pull the ball you just naturally hit more home runs. Another factor in there was the idea of self-preservation for the pitchers. You see, when they were pitching me outside I was hitting a lot of line drives through the box. I must have been getting a dozen pitchers a year with line drives, and they began thinking about that."

The league's big winner was Philadelphia's Robin Roberts with a 23–16 record, rung up over 347 innings of work. Adding luster to the tireless right-hander's performance was a run of 20 complete games from the start of the season until the Dodgers knocked him out on July 9, ending a string of 28 straight complete games dating back to the previous August 24.

Jim Gilliam may have been Rookie of the Year, but the Cardinals' first-year southpaw Harvey Haddix certainly was rookie pitcher of the year, winning 20 and losing 9, burnishing his record with a league-leading six shutouts.

"When we got together for the first time in spring training in 1953," Yankee pitcher Eddie Lopat recalled, "we all looked around at each other and said, 'One more time, huh?'"

And one more time it was, breaking all baseball records for dominance. For the New York Yankees, their fifth straight pennant in 1953 proved the easiest of the lot. After winning by margins of 1, 3, 5, and 2 games, Stengel's contingent of unbeatables outraced their pursuers by 8½ games, leaving Cleveland's Al Lopez in second place for the third consecutive year.

The Yankees occupied first place for 158 of the season's 167 days, including from May 11 to the end. On May 27, they went on a crushing victory binge that didn't end until June 14—18 straight wins, the final 14 scored on the road, where the club went on a Sherman-like march through Chicago, St. Louis, Detroit, and Cleveland. The Cleveland visit was a four-game sweep over Wynn, Feller, Lemon, and Garcia, which was the bluntest way of demoralizing their chief competitors. Needing just one more win to equal the league record of 19 straight set by the 1906 White Sox and matched by the 1947 edition of the Yankees, Stengel's marauders were beaten, ironically, by the cellar-ridden St. Louis Browns. It was a case of a pair of sudden, almost gravity-defying reversals: the Browns stopped the Yanks 18-game win streak with a victory that broke their own 14-game losing streak.

A few weeks later, the Yankees showed their human side with a 9-game losing streak that cut

Early Wynn.

Mickey Mantle.

The Milwaukee lumber company. *Left to right:* Joe Adcock, Sid Gordon, Eddie Mathews, Andy Pafko, Bill Bruton.

1·9·5·3

their lead from 12 games to 5. Thereafter, however, they played steadily, and when they clinched the pennant on September 14—two days after Brooklyn had done the same in the National League—they were 13 games in front.

Stengel's strong triumvirate of starters were beginning to show some age. Reynolds was thirty-eight (actually, doing more relieving than starting now), Lopat was thirty-five, and Raschi thirty-four. Still, they compiled a combined 32–17 won-lost record. The ace, however, was the twenty-four-year-old Whitey Ford. Fresh from military service, the skillful southpaw was 18–6 and on his way to the most scintillating mound career in Yankee annals.

The Yankee offense featured a couple of .300 hitters in Hank Bauer and Gene Woodling and the long ball from Mantle and Berra, and the longest ball of all from Mantle. It came on April 17, at Washington's Griffith Stadium. Batting against southpaw Chuck Stobbs, Mantle took a mighty swing and launched a mighty blow. The ball carried over the left-field bleachers and over the street behind the bleacher wall, and came to earth in an alley across the street. Measurement determined the ball had been airborne for some 565 feet. The shot established Mantle as one of the all-time long-distance hitters, bracketing him with such of the powerhouse elite as Babe Ruth and Jimmie Foxx, the recognized barons of the long, long home run.

The runner-up Indians had a few busters of their own, most notably third baseman Al Rosen, who turned in a sensational season that earned him a unanimous vote for Most Valuable Player. Rosen led the league with 43 home runs (one more than Philadelphia's Gus Zernial) and a whopping 145 runs batted in. Al missed the Triple Crown by a single batting point—his .336 being edged by Washington's Mickey Vernon's .337.

Cleveland's Larry Doby hit 29 homers and drove in 102 runs, but the free-swinging Doby also set a new American League record by striking out 121 times.

Cleveland's usually superb mound staff was not as effective as in past years. Bob Lemon was 21–15, Mike Garcia 18–9, and Early Wynn 17–12, while the declining Bob Feller was reduced to 10–7.

The White Sox finished a strong third, thanks primarily to the pitching of left-hander Billy Pierce (18–12) and righty Virgil Trucks, who was acquired from the Browns early in the season. Trucks was 15–6 with the Sox and had a combined record of 20–10. Two-time batting champion Ferris Fain, obtained from the Athletics, disappointed with a .256 batting average, but outfielder Minnie Minoso, one of the most popular players ever to perform for the White Sox, batted .313 and drove in 104 runs.

After 15 months in the Marine Corps, much of it spent in the war skies of Korea, Ted Williams returned to the Red Sox in August. It was a spectacular return for the premier slugger; getting into 37 games, Theodore hit 13 home runs, drove in 34 runs, and batted .407. Ted's belated return was one of the few bright spots for the fourth-place Red Sox, along with Billy Goodman's .313 average, George Kell's .307, and southpaw Mel Parnell's 21–8 record.

Along with Mickey Vernon's league-leading average, the fifth-place Senators also featured the league's most prolific winner in right-hander Bob Porterfield, whose 22–10 record was glitteringly inlaid with 9 shutouts, also tops.

The previous year's star American League pitcher, Philadelphia's Bobby Shantz, suffered an arm injury early in the season and was mired in a 5–9 season.

Detroit, a perennial breeding ground of .300 hitters, came up with another one in shortstop Harvey Kuenn. The American League's Rookie of the Year broke in with a .308 batting average and a league-high 209 hits. It was the beginning of a fine career for the line-drive-hitting Kuenn.

Also breaking in with the Tigers that year, albeit in just 30 games (batting .250), was an eighteen-year-old outfielder fresh out of high school named Al Kaline.

One of the most curious stories of the 1953 season, or of any season, for that matter, involved twenty-nine-year-old rookie right-hander Bobo Hollomon of the St. Louis Browns. On May 6, Hollomon pitched the pitcher's dream game, a no-hitter, against the Athletics. What made this particular gem unique was that it was Hollomon's debut as a major-league starter, marking the first and thus far only time a pitcher has coughed up a no-hitter in his first start. And what made the whole thing almost freakish was Hollomon's subsequent work. Bobo won just two more games and at the end of July, with a 3–7 record and 5.26 ERA, he was sent to the minor leagues, never to return to the bigs.

The 1953 World Series played out to what had become an October tradition—the Yankees rounding out their fifth straight pennant with their fifth straight world championship. The Dodgers carried Stengel's men to six games before being thwarted in a bid for their own first world title. What little joy Brooklyn fans derived from the October festivities came in the third game when Carl Erskine set a new Series record with 14 strikeouts in beating the Yankees 3–2.

World Series defeat or not, Brooklyn skipper Charlie Dressen felt he was sitting in the seat of advantage. No other Dodger manager had ever taken two pennants in a row, and the always ebullient, ever self-confident Charlie decided to dictate terms to the Dodger management. He would have the security of a three-year contract, he declared, or else. But the man he was trying to put the squeeze on was none other than Walter O'Malley, principal owner of the Dodgers, and not a man to be squeezed. Walter gave Charlie an ultimatum of his own—one year on the dotted line or nothing. Left dangling, all his cards called, Dressen had no recourse but to leave. He was replaced by a man who was, to the general public at least, an almost total unknown—Walter Alston, who had been managing successfully in the Dodger farm system. Alston was happy to settle for a one-year deal; in fact, before he retired in 1977, he had settled for 23 of them.

Roy Campanella.

Roy Campanella

There were two great catchers in the major leagues during the 1950s—the Yankees' Yogi Berra and the Dodgers' Roy Campanella. Each was a fine defensive player, each hit with power, and each was voted his league's Most Valuable Player three times in the first half of the decade (Berra in 1951, 1954, 1955, Campanella in 1951, 1953, 1955).

Campanella was born on November 19, 1921, in Philadelphia. He got his first professional experience playing in the Negro League, where he was watched covetously by scouts for the big-league clubs—clubs that were still unwilling to break the odious color barrier that was keeping blacks out of organized ball.

In 1946, however, Branch Rickey and the Brooklyn Dodgers began the dismantling of that barrier. When Jackie Robinson went to Montreal (then in the International League), Campanella and Don Newcombe were signed to contracts and assigned to the Class B Nashua, New Hampshire, team in the New England League. The following year, when Robinson became the first black to play in the major leagues, Roy was playing for Montreal. Although he was obviously big-league material, his promotion to the Dodgers was delayed for a few months in 1948 because Rickey wanted Roy to integrate the American Association with Brooklyn's St. Paul club.

"Mr. Rickey," the exasperated Campy said to the boss, "I'm no pioneer, I'm a ballplayer."

Nevertheless, he went. After playing 35 games at St. Paul, Campanella joined the Dodgers in Brooklyn. His genial personality, his flawless professionalism behind the plate, and the thunder in his bat made him an instant, and permanent, favorite in Ebbets Field.

Roy's greatest year was 1953, when he set records for catchers with 41 home runs and 142 runs batted in. (When Johnny Bench bettered both of those marks in 1970, he did so while playing some of his games in the outfield.)

He was the Rock of Gibraltar on the great Dodger teams of the 1950s, his squat, powerful body behind the plate "always a world of reassurance for us," as pitcher Johnny Podres said. Most catchers' visits to the mound were routine; but when Campy came out to talk to you, said Carl Erskine, "he always made you feel better, a little more confident."

A few months after his thirty-sixth birthday, Campanella was in an automobile accident that left him confined to a wheelchair for the rest of his life. It is a strong possibility that had this not happened, Campanella and not Frank Robinson might have been major-league baseball's first black manager.

Duke Snider.

Carl Erskine, 20–6 in 1953.

Brooklyn's Carl Furillo, the National League's leading hitter in 1953.

Brooklyn's wizard with the glove at third base, Billy Cox.

Whitey Ford.

Warren Spahn, 23–7 in 1953.

The Detroit Tigers have just added a brand-new rookie to their roster. Straight out of a Baltimore high school is eighteen-year-old Al Kaline *(left)*, being welcomed by skipper Fred Hutchinson. Twenty-two years and 3,007 hits later, Kaline retired.

Harvey Kuenn.

Washington first baseman Mickey Vernon, who took his second American League batting title in 1953 with a .337 average.

Bob Porterfield. The right-hander was the American League's top winner in 1953, with a 22–10 record, including 9 shutouts.

Chuck Stobbs, the Washington left-hander who served up Mantle's 565-foot home run. Otherwise, it wasn't a bad year for Chuck, who was 11–8.

Cardinals right-hander Gerry Staley, 18–9 in 1953.

Red Sox reliever Ellis Kinder, who had an excellent year in 1953. Appearing in 69 games, he won 10 and saved 27, with a 1.85 earned-run average.

Veteran right-hander Sid Hudson, who wound up his career with the Red Sox in the mid-1950s.

Dick Gernert, power-hitting Red Sox first baseman who hit 21 homers in 1953.

Mickey McDermott, the archetypical left-hander—colorful and with a smoking fast ball. He was 18–10 in 1953.

Boston's ace, Mel Parnell, 21–8 in 1953.

Harvey Haddix, 20–9 in his rookie year.

The Cardinals were expecting this big fellow to become a top home run slugger, but the best that first baseman Steve Bilko could do was 21 long shots in 1953.

Ralph Kiner, more accustomed to trotting his runs home, here comes in the hard way, sliding safely into Giants catcher Wes Westrum at the Polo Grounds.

Longtime Cardinals outfielder Enos Slaughter.

Dodger manager Charley Dressen.

Dodger first baseman Wayne Belardi. His problem was the team had another first baseman—Gil Hodges.

Dodger utility man Bobby Morgan.

Gil Hodges is out at home. Making the tag is Milwaukee's Del Crandall. Number 3 is Billy Cox. About to bring his thumb up is umpire Stan Landes.

Dodger pitcher Preacher Roe was legendary for his woeful hitting. But then came the big day—July 7, 1953, at Pittsburgh—when Preacher slammed a home run. His teammates marked the occasion by providing him with a carpet of towels on his way back to the dugout.

Dodger right-hander Billy Loes (14–8 in 1953) was called "moody," "eccentric," and other things. But Roy Campanella said all that mattered: "He has one of the best curve balls I've ever seen."

Jim Gilliam, Brooklyn's Rookie of the Year second baseman.

Brooklyn southpaw Johnny Podres. A rookie in 1953, Johnny broke in at 9–4.

Brooklyn right-hander Bob Milliken.

Cleveland's Al Rosen, the American League MVP in 1953.

The Cardinals' solid man at second base, Red Schoendienst. Red hit .342 in 1953.

Clint Courtney, the Browns' feisty catcher.

New York Giants third baseman Henry Thompson.

Right-hander Ike Delock, who pitched for the Red Sox through the 1950s.

Gus Zernial of the A's, who hit 42 homers in 1953.

1953 was a good year for Cincinnati's Gus Bell, who hit 30 homers, drove in 105 runs, and batted .300.

Bobo Holloman of the St. Louis Browns. A no-hitter in his first start, and then . . .

Gene Bearden, Cleveland's onetime ace left-hander, who was trying to hang on with the White Sox in 1953.

Chicago Cubs right-hander Johnny Klippstein.

The Cardinals' rookie third baseman Ray Jablonski, who broke in with a bang, hitting 21 homers and driving in 112 runs.

That's Brooklyn's Carl Furillo scoring against the Yankees in the second game of the 1953 World Series, just eluding Yogi Berra's diving tag. Bill Stewart is the umpire.

A view of the Polo Grounds during a Giant-Dodger game in July 1954.

1·9·5·4

For the National League, 1954 was the year of the return of Willie Mays and the year of the home run boomers. Six National Leaguers hit 40 or more home runs—Brooklyn's Gil Hodges (42) and Duke Snider (40), New York's Mays (41), Milwaukee's Eddie Mathews (40), Chicago's Hank Sauer (41), and the leader of them all, Cincinnati's Ted Kluszewski, who hammered 49 long ones and also led in runs batted in with 141. Curiously, after the 40 club, the drop-off was precipitous, with only Stan Musial getting into the thirties in home runs, with 35.

But the season belonged to Mays, back from two years in the Army and bursting into the league with the splendor and excitement that he was going to maintain for the better part of the next two decades. The delighted New York press tabbed him "Willie the Wonder" and "the Amazing Mays," and he was all of that.

There was nothing this twenty-three-year-old ballplaying marvel couldn't do on a ball field—and do better than anyone else—and he did it with a fervor and an enthusiasm that were infectious. Blazing his way to an MVP season, Mays, in addition to his 41 one-way tickets, led the league with a .345 batting average (winning out on the last day over teammate Don Mueller and Duke Snider), led in triples (13) and slugging (.667), and drove in 110 runs; all this in addition to covering the vast Polo Grounds center field with speed, skill, and a style that bordered on the theatrical.

With Mays back, it was another Dodger-Giant footrace to the finish, and this time Leo Durocher's club outraced the Dodgers under freshman skipper Walter Alston, winning by a comfortable five games.

Along with Mays and Mueller (who batted .342 and led with 212 hits), the Giants were still fielding some of the veterans of their 1951 "miracle" team—shortstop Alvin Dark, first baseman Whitey Lockman, third baseman

Henry Thompson, outfielder Monte Irvin, and catcher Wes Westrum.

Next to Mays, the Giants' most crucial new addition was left-hander Johnny Antonelli, obtained from the Braves in a swap for 1951 hero Bobby Thomson. It was a bad trade for the Braves, as Thomson broke an ankle in spring training and was out for most of the year. The injury, however, opened up a spot in the outfield for a twenty-year-old rookie just up from Jacksonville named Henry Aaron.

Antonelli shored up an aging Giant staff, winning 21 and losing 7, leading the league with a 2.29 ERA. Behind Johnny were right-hander Ruben Gomez, 17–9, the veteran Maglie at 14–6, and a pair of fine relief pitchers, Hoyt Wilhelm and veteran righty Marv Grissom.

Brooklyn's shot at a third straight pennant was sent astray by a year-long hand injury suffered by Roy Campanella. Unable to grip the bat with his normal strength, the two-time MVP saw his batting average drop 105 points to .207, his home runs from 41 to 19, and his RBIs from 142 to 51. Camp was picked up by Hodges and Snider, who in addition to their 40-home run seasons drove in 130 runs apiece. Brooklyn pitching was also under par in 1954. Carl Erskine, 1953's ace, labored through an 18–15 season, and no other Dodger pitcher won more than 13. Don Newcombe, returning after two years in the service, was a disappointment with a 9–8 record.

After a slow start, the Giants reached first place on June 9 and were never headed thereafter, using a 24–4 June record as their springboard.

Flexing their muscles in third place (with three 10-game winning streaks along the way) were the Milwaukee Braves. It would be three more years before the Braves took a pennant, but they were setting things in order. Their big man was Mathews with his 40 homers and 103

1·9·5·4

runs batted in. Behind Eddie was first baseman Joe Adcock, who clubbed 23 home runs, including 9 at Ebbets Field (tying the road record for homers against a single club). On July 31, Big Joe put on a truly devastating performance in Brooklyn. On that afternoon he became only the second National Leaguer since 1900 to hit 4 home runs in a nine-inning game (Gil Hodges was the first). Joe also had a double (his weakness that day), giving him a record 18 total bases and a record-tying 5 extra-base hits in one game.

Adcock's power display was no fluke; the year before, on April 29, he had become the first man ever to drive one into the center-field bleachers at the Polo Grounds, a belt of some 480 feet.

Behind Mathews and Adcock, the Braves had shortstop Johnny Logan, catcher Del Crandall, and outfielders Bill Bruton, Andy Pafko, and young Aaron, who broke in with 13 home runs and a .280 batting average. Warren Spahn won 21 games, making him a six-time 20-game winner, the first National League lefty ever to achieve this plateau.

It was another Milwaukee pitcher who delivered the major leagues' only no-hitter in 1954. Right-hander Jim Wilson had been languishing in the bullpen when a back injury suffered by pitcher Gene Conley put Wilson into the rotation. In his first start, on June 6, Jim pitched a shutout. That was but a warm-up for his big one on June 12, when he fired a no-hitter against the Phillies. For Wilson the achievement had a particular sweetness, for twice in previous years his career had been put in jeopardy when he was shot off the mound by line drives, once suffering a skull fracture and once a broken leg. Overall, Wilson was 8–2 for the year, with four shutouts.

The league's big winner on the mound for the third straight year, and for the fifth straight a 20-game winner, was Robin Roberts, with a 23–15 record. On a roll of a different sort was Roberts's teammate, right-hander Murry Dickson, obtained over the winter from Pittsburgh. With the Pirates, Dickson had led the league in losses in 1952 and 1953, and with the Phillies he managed to achieve this unwanted distinction again with a 10–20 record.

For the St. Louis Cardinals it was a most frustrating season. Finishing out of the first division for only the second time in 16 years, the Cards ran sixth despite leading the league with a .281 team batting average. The club had four .300 hitters in Red Schoendienst (.315), Rookie of the Year outfielder Wally Moon (.304), catcher Bill Sarni (.300), and the inevitable Stan Musial (.330).

On May 2, Musial put on a one-man slugging show against the Giants in a doubleheader at Busch Stadium (formerly Sportsman's Park) in St. Louis. Although leading the league at one time or another in every offensive department, Musial never led in home runs. In that May 2 doubleheader, however, Stanley dazzled the hometown customers by hitting three homers in the first game and two in the second, the five bell-ringers setting a record for homers in a doubleheader (since tied by San Diego's Nate Colbert in 1972). "I was just swinging for base hits the way I always do," the modest Musial said later. "The only time I was consciously going for a home run was in my last at bat in the second game." He popped up.

Sinking the hard-hitting Cardinals that year was their starting pitching. Beyond Harvey Haddix (18–13) and right-hander Brooks Lawrence (15–6), there was little that manager Eddie Stanky was able to bring out to the mound. The Cardinals had acquired onetime Yankee ace Vic Raschi in the spring, but Big Vic was looking at the downhill side now and finished with an 8–9 record. Raschi made the trivia lists, however, when one of his April deliveries became Henry Aaron's first major-

1·9·5·4

league home run—the first of 755.

The most sizzling mound debut of the year was made by Dodger left-hander Karl Spooner. With the Giants having already wrapped things up, the Dodgers called Spooner up from their Fort Worth farm club and on September 22 put him on the mound against the Giants at Ebbets Field. The hard-throwing youngster shut out the National League champs on 3 hits and fanned 15—breaking by 2 the previous record for a pitcher in his first start. Four days later, in the final game of the season, Spooner shut out the Pirates 1–0 on 4 hits and struck out 12. The rookie's 27 strikeouts in two consecutive games was a record (breaking Dazzy Vance's record by 2); also, he became only the second National League pitcher to break in with a pair of shut-outs (the Giants' Allan Worthington had done it just the year before).

Measuring Spooner's late-season heroics against their club's second-place finish, Dodger fans went into the long winter muttering, "We shoulda had Spooner sooner."

In the American League what did not happen was more remarkable than what did: For the first time since 1948, someone other than the New York Yankees won the pennant.

Three straight second-place finishes had made the Cleveland Indians more resolute than ever, and in 1954 they finally found the way to derail the Yankee express—win more games than any team in American League history ever had. Al Lopez's club won 111 games (topping the old record set by the 1927 Yankees by one).

One might have thought that a team winning 111 games (in a 154-game schedule and play-ing .721 ball) would have rolled to the pennant perspiration-free; but this was not the case, even though the Indians' final margin over the Yankees was 8 games. As late as September 5, the second-place Yankees were just 3½ games

back. Casey Stengel's five-time winners were resolved not to let go of the torch without a struggle. They won 103 games, more than any Stengel-led team ever had or would, a number exceeded only seven times in league history, a number that would have guaranteed a pennant almost any other time.

The 1954 season, however, was not a nor-mal time in the American League. Seldom has a league ever demonstrated so extreme an imbal-ance as this one did in 1954. The talent was so stacked at the top that the first three teams—Cleveland, New York, and Chicago—won the same amount of games, 308, as did the other five teams.

On September 12, the Yankees, trailing the Indians by 6½, were in Cleveland for a double-header. In front of 86,583 people—at the time the largest crowd ever to see a baseball game—Lemon and Wynn put the Yanks away by scores of 4–1 and 3–2, and for all intents and purposes ended the race right there.

Cleveland pitching, for years considered to be baseball's elite corps, was never stronger or deeper than in 1954. Bob Lemon, who always seemed to be first among equals, was 23–7, while Early Wynn was 23–11, and Mike Garcia 19–8. Behind the Big Three were Art Houtte-man (15–7), Bob Feller (13–3), and a righty-lefty bullpen tandem in Ray Narleski and Don Mossi that was superb all year.

Cleveland's batting attack was led by second baseman Bobby Avila, the league's leading hit-ter with a .341 batting average; third baseman Al Rosen, with a .300 batting average and 102 runs batted in; and outfielder Larry Doby, who led the league with 32 home runs and 126 runs batted in.

On their way to becoming only the second American League team to win 100 games and not take the pennant (the 1915 Tigers won 100 and finished second), the Yankees saw some of their Gibraltars of the mound finally begin to

1·9·5·4

feel the years winding tightly around them. Eddie Lopat, thirty-six years old, and Allie Reynolds, thirty-nine, won just 25 games between them. And Vic Raschi was gone, having been traded to the Cardinals after a contract dispute with George Weiss. Some of the slack was picked up by 20-game-winning Rookie of the Year Bob Grim, while Whitey Ford delivered another good year (16–8).

The Yankees had four .300 hitters in the lineup: third baseman Andy Carey (.302), MVP catcher Yogi Berra (.307), and outfielders Mickey Mantle (.300) and Irv Noren (.319), plus rookie part-timer Bill Skowron, who broke into 87 games and batted .340.

With a bench that included solid players like Gene Woodling, Bob Cerv, Jerry Coleman, Bobby Brown, Enos Slaughter, and Eddie Robinson, Stengel platooned and juggled all year, using a record 262 pinch hitters, who responded with an excellent .292 batting average. But 111 Cleveland wins were just too many to overcome.

Chicago's Minnie Minoso delivered another fine year with a .320 batting average, 116 RBIs, and a league-high 18 triples, while teammate Nelson Fox batted .319. White Sox right-hander Virgil Trucks was 19–12, heading a good staff that included 16-game winners Sandy Consuegra and Bob Keegan. The Chisox won 94 games, remarkably high for a third-place club.

It was actually Ted Williams and not Bobby Avila who had the highest batting average in the league that season, although Avila won the title, and thereby hangs a tale of a rules change. Under then current rules, a batter had to have a total of 477 official plate appearances to qualify for the batting title. Avila more than qualified with 555, but Williams had only 386. Williams, however, was walked 136 times. Noting the injustice of this, the rules committee effected a change from official times at bat to plate

appearances. The change came too late to award Williams (who batted .345 to Avila's .341), but the rule remains on the books to this day. (Under the 162-game schedule, a qualifying batting champion needs 502 plate appearances.)

Added to Williams's disappointing loss of another batting crown was the pain and frustration of serious injury. Diving for a fly ball on the first day of spring training, Ted broke a collarbone. The injury kept him out of the lineup until May 16. When he returned, it was in grand style. Making his 1954 debut in a doubleheader in Detroit, the great slugger collected eight hits in nine tries, including two home runs.

Detroit's 1953 Rookie of the Year, shortstop Harvey Kuenn, made wet bread of the "sophomore jinx" by again batting .300 (.306) and again leading in hits with 201.

Following the success of the Boston Braves' move to Milwaukee, another major-league franchise shift took place. The St. Louis Browns, long-suffering in the standings and at the gate, were sold to a syndicate that immediately moved the club to Baltimore, where they opened the 1954 season. Baltimore, an original American League city, had left the league in 1902, when its franchise moved to New York. Now big-league baseball was back, and like the Braves in Milwaukee, the Orioles in Baltimore were received by enthusiastic fans who came to the ball park in large numbers. In their final year in St. Louis, the club had drawn under 300,000; in their first year in Baltimore, attendance shot up to over a million. These intoxicating numbers were not going unnoticed; indeed, they were like beckoning fingers to all restless and disenchanted club owners. The era of the unmoored franchise and ultimately of expansion in major-league baseball had begun.

Despite all the clamor, Baltimore finished seventh in the eight-team league. The Orioles did have one highly attractive piece of mer-

1·9·5·4

chandise, a twenty-three-year-old right-hander named Bob Turley. Called "Bullet Bob" for the speed of his fast ball, young Turley was, in the tradition of neophyte fireballers, fast and wild. With a 14–15 record, he led in strikeouts with 185 and bases on balls with 181. All it would take to make a first-rank pitcher of Turley was to harness that speed and give it a semblance of control. Every club in the league was licking its lips in hopes of getting the opportunity to do just that, for Bullet Bob was going to be made available.

Baltimore's brand-new general manager Paul Richards had decided that the only way to give his struggling team a fast fix and keep those hordes of customers pointed in the right direction was to trade Turley for as many good players as he could. There was only one club with the talent to spare: the Yankees. Accordingly, on November 18, 1954, the Yankees and Orioles made the first part of what was to be a massive 18-player deal. The Yankees received Turley, right-hander Don Larsen (only 3–21, but with an intriguing assortment of stuff), and shortstop Billy Hunter; the Orioles received pitchers Harry Byrd and Jim McDonald, shortstop Willie Miranda, catchers Hal Smith and Gus Triandos (both fine prospects made superfluous by Berra), and outfielder Gene Woodling. On December 1, four more Orioles (of little distinction) were shipped to

New York in exchange for four more Yankees (also of little distinction). Of all the players involved, only Turley and Larsen in New York and Triandos in Baltimore were going to have significant impact on their new clubs.

There was another large movement of players made after the season—this time the entire club, as the owners of the Philadelphia Athletics received permission to move Connie Mack's old club to Kansas City, citing the old bugaboo, declining attendance, the A's having barely cleared the 300,000 mark in turnstile spins in 1954. With the A's having finished in the second division for the nineteenth time in 21 years, more than a few of their fans were willing to help the club pack its bags.

The 1954 World Series was a startling show, dominated by Willie Mays, whose sensational running catch in the opening game saved it for the Giants, and pinch hitter Dusty Rhodes, whose timely swats contributed to three of the four Giant victories. The Cleveland Indians, after setting a record with 111 wins during the season, went into the winter with those same 111 wins after being wiped out in four by the Giants.

Cleveland skipper Al Lopez gave his thoughts on the Series:

"They say anything can happen in a short series. Well, I knew that. I just never thought it was going to be *that* short."

Willie Mays.

Bobby Thomson may have hit the home run in the 1951 pennant playoff with the Dodgers that gave the Giants the National League championship, but it was Willie Mays who had made the difference all season long. Joining a struggling Giant team in late May (coming up from Minneapolis, where he was batting a resounding .477), Willie was like a buoyant transfusion. Playing center field with a dash and verve that amazed opponents and stimulated teammates, throwing out base runners with as powerful an arm as there was in baseball, and delivering clutch hits throughout the summer, Willie "made the difference."

The ebullient youngster with the high-pitched giggle and the habit of calling everyone "Say-hey" was born in Westfield, Alabama, on May 6, 1931. Growing up in this Birmingham suburb, Willie was encouraged by his father, Willie senior, to play ball, and by the time the boy was seventeen he was playing professionally alongside his father for the Birmingham Black Barons in the Negro League.

Scouted and bypassed by several clubs, Mays was seen in the spring of 1950 by Giant scout Eddie Montague, who was absolutely dazzled by the youngster and strongly urged his employers to sign him. Willie was soon on his way to the Trenton, New Jersey, club of the Class B Interstate League. After batting .353 there and his notable .477 at Minneapolis, Mays began a career in the big leagues that stretched from 1951 to 1973.

In the opinion of many who watched Mays starting out, he was to become the greatest of modern-day ballplayers, the most complete talent since DiMaggio. It wasn't just that Mays was without fault on a baseball diamond, it was that his many talents and qualities were of supernova magnitude. A man who within a few years' time leads the league in batting, home runs, triples, stolen bases, total bases, slugging percentage, and outfield assists is more of a planet than a star.

As much a part of the Mays legend as his playing talent was the carbonation in his personality and the salutary effect it had on his teammates. Branch Rickey described it as Willie's "secret weapon," saying that "Willie Mays has doubled his strength with laughter."

Mays's 660 lifetime home runs have slotted him third on the all-time scroll, behind Aaron's 755 and Ruth's 714. Sometimes overlooked in the considerations of Willie's records are the two seasons he lost to military service in the early part of his career (most of 1952 and all of 1953). If not for that lost time, it would in all probability have been Willie's home run record rather than Ruth's that Henry Aaron broke in 1974.

Bob Lemon.

Mike Garcia.

Dusty Rhodes, who batted .341 as a part-timer for the Giants in 1954 and kept right on hitting in the World Series.

Monte Irvin, outfielder with the 1954 Giants.

Giants outfielder Don Mueller, who batted .342 in 1954.

Ted Kluszewski, who hit 49 homers and drove in 141 runs in 1954.

Nelson Fox.

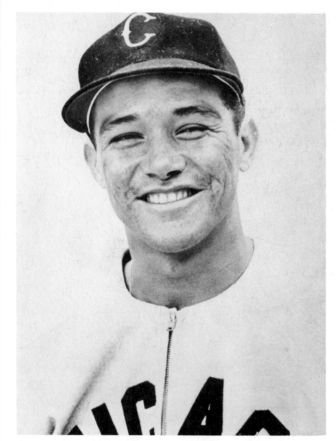

Chico Carrasquel, the White Sox' regular shortstop until the arrival of Luis Aparicio in 1956.

The Yankees' rookie first baseman Bill Skowron, who hit .340 as a part-timer in his rookie season. (Photo by Bob Olen.)

On July 31, 1956, Milwaukee's Joe Adcock hit four home runs and a double against the Dodgers at Ebbets Field. The next day, Joe was hit in the head with a pitched ball. Here he is showing Milwaukee manager Charlie Grimm the dent the ball made in Joe's batting helmet.

Ted Williams.

Cleveland's right-handed relief ace Ray Narleski.

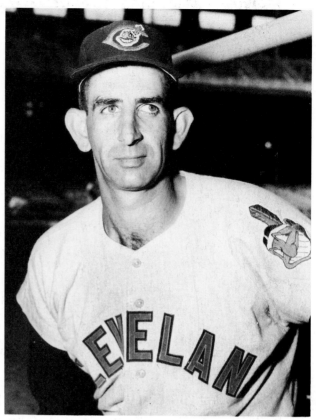

Cleveland's left-handed relief ace Don Mossi.

Cleveland's Larry Doby, who led the American League in home runs and runs batted in in 1954.

Cleveland Stadium, home of the Indians.

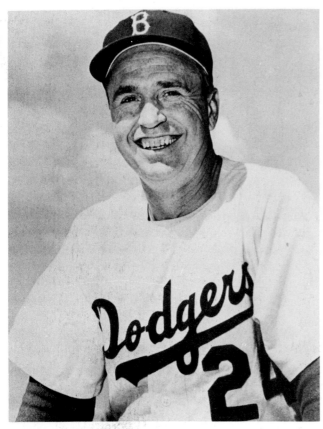

Walter Alston.

Dodger outfielder Walt Moryn. He later played for the Cubs, for whom he had some fine years.

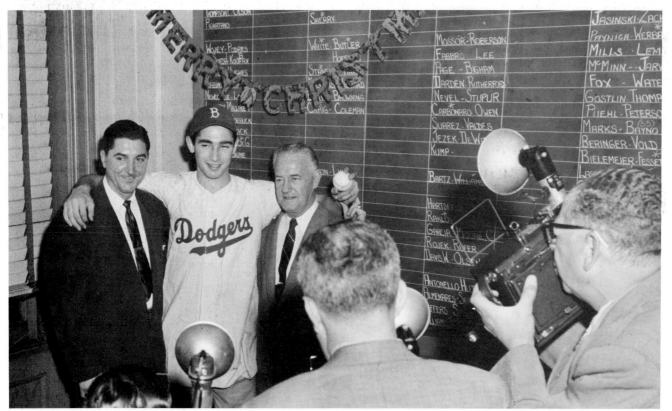

It's a few days before Christmas in 1954, and the Dodgers are holding a press conference to announce the signing of a young, left-handed bonus baby. His name is Sandy Koufax. Here he is posing with Dodger executives Al Campanis *(left)* and Fresco Thompson.

Wally Moon, the Cardinals' Rookie of the Year in 1954.

St. Louis Cardinal right-hander Brooks Lawrence.

Outfielder Sam Mele, who moved about quite a bit in the 1950s, playing for the Senators, White Sox, Orioles, Red Sox, Reds, and Indians.

Giants right-hander Ruben Gomez.

Paul Richards, who managed the White Sox and Orioles in the 1950s.

Jim Hughes, right-handed relief pitcher for the Dodgers.

Cleveland outfielder Dave Philley.

Brooklyn pitchers Carl Erskine *(left)* and Karl Spooner.

Dave Pope, utility outfielder with the Cleveland Indians.

Gene Conley, Milwaukee's tall right-hander. A gifted athlete, Conley also played basketball for the Boston Celtics.

Aerial view of Wrigley Field, home of the Chicago Cubs.

Cincinnati Reds second baseman Johnny Temple, who batted .307 in 1954. *(Courtesy of the Cincinnati Reds.)*

Cincinnati's Jim Greengrass. The slugging outfielder hit 27 homers in 1954. *(Courtesy of the Cincinnati Reds.)*

Joe DiMaggio and bride Marilyn Monroe. They were married in 1954, divorced a year later.

Milwaukee right-hander Dave Jolly. Dave had a good year coming in from the bullpen, with an 11–6 record.

Danny O'Connell, Milwaukee second baseman.

Right-hander Bob Grim, the Yankees' 20-game-winning Rookie of the Year in 1954.

New York Yankee third baseman Andy Carey, who hit .302 in 1954.

Giants left fielder Monte Irvin *(left)* and shortstop Alvin Dark ganging up on a fly ball.

Yankee infielder Irv Noren, who batted .319 in 1954.

Walker Cooper, veteran National League catcher who caught for the Reds, Braves, Pirates, Cubs, and Cardinals in the 1950s.

Southpaw Dick Littlefield, who took the grand tour in the 1950s, pitching for the Red Sox, White Sox, Tigers, Browns, Orioles, Pirates, Cardinals, Giants, Cubs, and Braves.

Detroit second baseman Frank Bolling.

Red Sox shortstop Milt Bolling, brother of Detroit's Frank.

Cleveland's Jim Hegan, considered by many the top defensive catcher of his time.

The two league batting champions meeting before the first game of the 1954 World Series. Cleveland's Bobby Avila *(left)* and the Giants' Willie Mays.

The fabled Mays catch in the first game of the 1954 World Series at the Polo Grounds. It came in the top of the eighth inning of a 2–2 tie, with two men on base and none out. The 460-foot drive was hit by Vic Wertz, who was to say wryly in later years, "Willie made me famous."

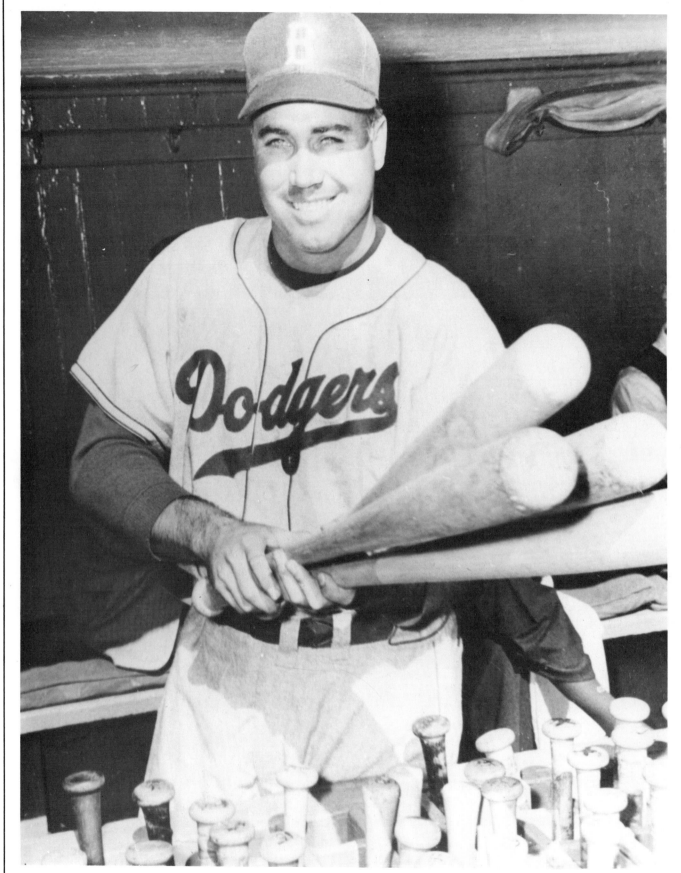

Duke Snider, who had 42 home runs and 136 runs batted in for the Dodgers in 1955.

1·9·5·5

Those who had expected freshman manager Walter Alston to be canned after failing to win the pennant in 1954 were not yet acquainted with Dodger president Walter O'Malley's loyalty toward skippers he liked. Alston stayed on (and on and on), vindicating the boss's confidence in him as the Dodgers took all suspense out of the 1955 pennant race early and emphatically.

The Dodgers began the season with a high-octane leap from the starting block; it was, in fact, a record-smashing high-octane leap. Alston's men began burning the bridges behind them as they won their first 10 games, breaking the record for starting-gate victories of 9, held by the 1918 Giants, 1940 Dodgers, and 1944 St. Louis Browns (who had some help from World War II). After losing 2 of their next 3, the Dodgers inhaled mightily and swept their next 11. On May 10, their record stood out with neon splendor: 22–2. After that, it was merely a matter of maintaining pulsebeats to assure their pennant.

On June 21 the Dodgers were 14 games ahead, in early July they slumped to 11½, but by August 16 they had soared to 16½ ahead of second-place Milwaukee, which is like having "Go Away" written on your welcome mat. On September 8, the day they clinched the pennant in Milwaukee, the Brooks held a 17-game lead. The September 8 date marked the earliest pennant lock in National League history.

The Dodgers won their pennant with some rousing year-long slugging—leading the league in home runs and slugging percentage for the seventh straight year—and a solid pitching staff that led in strikeouts for the eighth year in a row, and in earned-run average.

Brooklyn hit 201 home runs, led by top crashers Duke Snider (42), Roy Campanella (32), Gil Hodges (27), and Carl Furillo (26). Snider, Hodges, and Campanella each drove in over 100 runs, with the Duke leading the league

with 136. For Campanella, recovered from his hand injury of the year before, it was a third MVP season.

The pitching was headed by Don Newcombe, who put together a superb 20–5 season. In addition to his mound dominance, the big right-hander also set a new league record for pitchers by hitting seven home runs, breaking the old mark of six set by the Giants' Hal Schumacher in 1934 and equaled by Boston's Jim Tobin in 1942. Used as a pinch hitter throughout the season (he was 8-for-21), Newk batted .359, and at times made the Dodgers look like a one-man band.

Following Newcombe in the rotation were Carl Erskine, Billy Loes, Roger Craig, and lefty Johnny Podres. Alston also had a strong bullpen with right-handers Clem Labine, Ed Roebuck, and Don Bessent. Karl Spooner, the exciting rookie of a year before, started and relieved and had an 8–6 record. A sore arm was soon to deprive the gifted young southpaw of what promised to be a brilliant career.

Because of then-existing rules stipulating that a team keep on its roster all season any player receiving a bonus in excess of $6,000, the Dodgers carried on the rolls another hard-throwing young left-hander. He was a seldom-used nineteen-year-old named Sandy Koufax. Destined to become one of the greatest pitchers in baseball history, the young man broke in with a 2–2 record, with both victories shutouts.

Second-place Milwaukee showed impressive power with 182 home runs, Eddie Mathews hitting 41 of them, young Henry Aaron 27, and catcher Del Crandall 26. Milwaukee's other big socker, Joe Adcock, missed the second half of the season after suffering a broken arm when struck by a pitched ball. The twenty-one-year-old Aaron, beginning his long climb to the all-time home run record, drove in 106 runs and batted .314, establishing himself after just two years as one of the league's premier hitters.

1·9·5·5

The Braves suffered another debilitating loss when right-hander Gene Conley, 11–5 at the All-Star break, developed an ailing shoulder and failed to win another game for the rest of the season.

Willie Mays gave the third-place Giants another season of pageantry and spectacle. New York's incomparable center fielder hit a prodigious 51 homers, becoming after Hack Wilson, Ralph Kiner (twice), and Johnny Mize only the fourth National Leaguer to clear the half-century mark in home runs. In addition to all those home runs and his usual stellar defensive play, Willie batted .319 and drove in 127 runs, and for the second year in a row led in triples (13). He also led in slugging (.659) and missed the stolen-base crown by one—24 to Milwaukee's Bill Bruton's 25. The stolen base was still a seldom-employed offensive weapon, and would remain so until 1962, when Maury Wills startled everyone with 104 swipes—more than double what any National Leaguer had done since 1920—and revived the forgotten art of base stealing.

Leo Durocher's pitching, so strong the year before in hurling the team to the pennant, underwent a sharp decline in 1955. The ace, Johnny Antonelli, dropped from 21–7 to 14–16, while Ruben Gomez and Sal Maglie experienced similar drop-offs. Maglie, in fact, was waived out of the league to the Cleveland Indians late in the season.

The Phillies finished fourth despite outstanding seasons from Robin Roberts and outfielder Richie Ashburn. A 20-game winner for the sixth year in a row, Roberts was 23–14, leading National League pitchers in victories for the fourth time running, and working over 300 innings for the sixth straight year. Ashburn, the club's speedy center fielder, won the batting title with a .338 average.

Cincinnati, putting together one of the league's more potent lineups, hit 181 home runs but still finished fifth because of one of baseball's venerable hard-luck stories—spotty pitching. Big Ted Kluszewski followed his 49–home run season with 47 long ones, followed by outfielder Wally Post's 40 and outfielder Gus Bell's 27. Each of these power boys drove in over 100 runs. Bell, whose son Buddy was to become a great third baseman several decades later, had developed into one of the league's most feared hitters.

The National League, already boasting most of baseball's brightest stars, saw the emergence of another lusty, first-magnitude slugger in 1955. His name was Ernie Banks and he played shortstop for the Chicago Cubs, and hit most uncharacteristically for a shortstop. In only his second full year, Banks hit 44 home runs, batted .295, and drove in 117 runs. His accomplishments that season included a new major-league record—5 grand-slam home runs in a single season.

With stars like Banks, Mays, Aaron, Jackie Robinson, Campanella, and Newcombe, the National League was reaping the harvest of having moved more quickly to sign black players than the American League. The social revolution begun in 1947, when Branch Rickey brought Jackie Robinson to Brooklyn to integrate major-league baseball, was now eminently successful, irreversible, and rapidly expanding—but more so in the National League than in the American, where clubs like Boston and Detroit had yet to field their first black player, even as the New York Yankees had waited until 1955 to do so.

Banks's 44 home runs were the most ever by a shortstop. Ernie's teammate, right-hander Sam Jones, uncorked the year's only no-hitter, shutting down the Pirates on May 12. Sam made it dramatic in the top of the ninth when he walked the first three batters to face him; but then, facing the heart of the Pittsburgh lineup, he bore down and struck out Dick Groat,

1·9·5·5

Roberto Clemente, and Frank Thomas.

Clemente was a twenty-year-old rookie out-fielder that season, having been drafted out of the Brooklyn organization for $10,000. Roberto broke in quietly with a .255 batting average, but attracted admiring attention with his running speed and laser-beam throwing arm.

The Pirates were slowly putting together the team that five years later would take the world championship. Clemente was there, and so were shortstop Dick Groat and pitchers Vernon Law, Bob Friend, and Roy Face. It was Law who on July 19 put on a unique iron-man performance against the Braves at Pittsburgh's Forbes Field. Law hurled the first 18 innings of a 19-inning game, the last 14 of them scoreless. In the bottom of the eighteenth, Pirate manager Fred Haney lifted Law for a pinch hitter "to save Law's arm." (One wonders what Fred had been thinking about up until then.) Bob Friend came in, gave up a run in the top of the nineteenth, but then became the winning pitcher when the Pirates came back with two in the bottom of the inning. Friend had a 14–9 record that year with the last-place Pirates and led the league with a 2.84 ERA, becoming the first pitcher ever to win an ERA title with a last-place club.

The Cardinals finished in seventh place, their lowest terminal point since 1919. The only glory that came to St. Louis in 1955, besides Stan Musial's .319 batting average and the sharp play of rookie third baseman Ken Boyer, was having the league's Rookie of the Year for the second year in a row. Following Wally Moon in 1954 was outfielder Bill Virdon, who batted .281.

In mid-August, Brooklyn Dodger president Walter O'Malley announced that his club would play seven of its home games in Jersey City in 1956 and that it was also his intention to abandon the antiquated Ebbets Field after 1957 to play in a new stadium yet to be built. With his stunning team slated to draw just over one million customers, O'Malley pointed to the park's age (it opened in 1913), its modest seating capacity (around 32,000), and its inadequate parking facilities. Some people thought the manipulative Dodger owner was trying to exert subtle pressure to get the city to build a new stadium for him. This may have been true; but what was also happening was that O'Malley had paced off the first mile of the move that two years later would take the Dodgers (and the Giants) out of New York and relocate them on the West Coast.

In contrast to Brooklyn's high-speed rush through the National League, the American League put on a razzle-dazzle pennant race. As late as the morning of September 8, a tight, three-game blanket covered the Yankees, Indians, White Sox, and Red Sox.

With September the key month, the Yankees caught fire and played at a 17–6 pace, followed by Cleveland's 14–9, Chicago's 12–12, and Boston's 10–14. The Yankee stretch drive gave Casey Stengel his sixth pennant in seven years, the New Yorkers coming home three ahead of Cleveland and five ahead of Chicago.

The Yankees benefited from the first truly big season of Mickey Mantle's career. The gifted switch hitter took his first home run title with a total of 37, comfortably ahead of Kansas City's Gus Zernial, who hit 30. (Contrast this with the National League, where six men hit 40 or more.) Mickey's .306 batting average made him Stengel's only full-timer to clear the .300 mark.

Nevertheless, Stengel had plenty of talent on the club, and he handled it skillfully. Elston Howard, the team's first black player, broke into 97 games (most of them in the outfield) and batted .290. (Upon congratulating themselves on hiring a black player for the first time—it was now eight years after the arrival of Jackie Robinson—the Yankees stressed that

1·9·5·5

Howard was "dignified" and a "gentleman." Howard was certainly both of these, but it was the first time that either quality seems to have been weighed alongside a man's ability to hit, run, throw, and field.)

Stengel's rock of stability continued to be Yogi Berra behind the plate. Catching 145 games, Berra batted .272, hit 27 home runs, and drove in 108 runs, all of which earned him his third Most Valuable Player plaque.

It was a year in which the American League was a bit light on high-quality pitching—for the first time in its 55-year history, the league failed to produce a 20-game winner. Or a 19-game winner, for that matter. The top winners were three 18-gamers: New York's Whitey Ford (18–7), Cleveland's Bob Lemon (18–10), and Boston's Frank Sullivan (18–13).

Bob Turley, the pivotal man in the Yankees' 18-man swap with the Orioles, backed up Ford with a 17–13 season, while southpaw Tommy Byrne was 16–5. What Stengel had done was rebuild his pitching staff while fighting for a pennant. Allie Reynolds had retired the previous winter, and Eddie Lopat fell to a 4–8 record and was traded to Baltimore in mid-season. Also, 1954's 20-game-winning rookie Bob Grim had a bad arm and was reduced to a 7–5 season. Stengel, however, made up the difference with Turley, the veteran Byrne, Don Larsen (9–2), and thirty-eight-year-old reliever Jim Konstanty, picked up from the National League the previous September.

While there weren't any no-hitters in the American League in 1955, Whitey Ford turned in a couple of performances that were like little brothers to Johnny Vander Meer's double no-hit games of 1938. The Yankee southpaw, on September 2 and again on September 7, pitched successive one-hitters against Washington and Kansas City. Ford was the first American League pitcher ever to throw back-to-back one-hitters; in the National League, only two

pitchers had done it since 1900—Chicago's Lon Warneke in 1934 and St. Louis' Mort Cooper in 1943.

There was another notable one-hitter in the league that year. Though winning only four games in this, his penultimate season, Bob Feller made one of them his twelfth career one-hitter, a major-league record and a remarkable one. The thirty-six-year-old Cleveland legend delivered his gem against the Red Sox on May 5.

Given as the prime reason for Cleveland's failure to repeat was the slightly reduced efficiency of the club's Big Three pitchers. Lemon was 18–10, Wynn 17–11, and Garcia 16–10; solid seasons for each, but it added up to 51–31 as compared to 1954's 65–26.

But Cleveland also brought into the league that year what everyone agreed was one of the most spectacular young pitching prospects ever to come to the big leagues. He was twenty-two-year-old left-hander Herb Score, the American League's Rookie of the Year. Greatness had been predicted for him from the moment he was signed (by the same scout who had signed Bob Feller for the club, Cy Slapnicka), and greatness he delivered. In his first season the tall, trim young southpaw was 16–10, firing a blazing fast ball and backbreaking curve that helped him record a league-leading 245 strikeouts, which set a new rookie record, one that stood until the Mets' Dwight Gooden eclipsed it in 1984.

Two of Cleveland's top hitters also took slides in 1955, much more precipitous than the pitching. Batting champ Bobby Avila dipped from .341 to .272 and Al Rosen from .300 to .244. Also hurting Cleveland's shot at repeating was the illness that beset hard-hitting first baseman Vic Wertz in late August, a nonparalytic type of polio that sidelined him for the rest of the season.

Coming in third for the fourth straight year

1·9·5·5

were the Chicago White Sox. The Sox had a pair of .300 hitters in third baseman George Kell (.312) and sparkplug second baseman Nelson Fox (.311), while southpaw Billy Pierce was the ERA leader with an impressive 1.97.

Through June and July the Red Sox were the league's hottest team, racking up a 41–17 record. But mediocre performances in the first and last thirds of the season doomed the Bosox to a fourth-place windup. The club had two serious handicaps during the season. The first was caused when Ted Williams was late in reporting because of marital difficulties. Getting into 98 games, he batted .356, falling short of qualifying for the batting title.

The second blow to the Red Sox was a personal tragedy. Their highly talented young first baseman Harry Agganis was hospitalized early in the season by pneumonia; and then, suddenly, on June 27, the twenty-five-year-old athlete died of a blood clot. A brilliant career had been forecast for the former Boston University quarterback who had chosen baseball as his career. In 1954, Agganis broke in with a .254 batting average; in 1955, he was batting .313 when he took ill and died.

The most surprising player in the league in 1955 was Detroit's twenty-year-old outfielder Al Kaline. Playing only his second full season, the youngster displayed the large-sized talent that was going to make him one of the game's most consistent stars for the next two decades. Kaline batted .340, and no one in the league did better, making him the youngest player ever to win a batting title. Al salted his fine season with 27 home runs, 102 runs batted in, and a league-leading 200 hits. Additional punch was added to the Tiger lineup by Harvey Kuenn, with a .306 batting average, and third baseman Ray Boone, whose 116 runs batted in tied him for the lead with Boston's Jackie Jensen.

Another success story took place in Kansas City, though this one was financial rather than artistic. Duplicating the smashing success enjoyed by the transplanted Braves and Browns, the newly ordained Kansas City Athletics drew nearly 1,400,000 fans, an astonishing leap from the 304,000 the club had seated the year before in Philadelphia. And all the more astonishing when one considers that this was a standard sixth-place team. It was further evidence of the need, and inevitability, of big-league expansion.

The Brooklyn Dodgers, who had started the season at high speed, continued going, right on through the World Series. In a pulsating seven-game encounter with the Yankees, Alston's club took their first championship ever when Johnny Podres shut out the Yankees in the seventh game 2–0. Brooklyn's championship, it developed, turned on a sensational running catch made by left-fielder Sandy Amoros in the sixth inning of the finale, a catch that began a double play that snuffed out a Yankee rally and sent the Dodgers on to the only championship they would ever win in Brooklyn.

During the winter meetings, the directors of the National League clubs voted to make protective headgear mandatory for all batters, formalizing an innovation that had been introduced by Branch Rickey in Pittsburgh a few years before. The vote was 6–2. Why did two clubs vote against the wearing of helmets, which in years to come were to save many players from serious injury, and maybe even save a few lives? Well, why were many major-league clubs initially against the broadcasting of their games? Why were certain owners positive that night ball would be a "passing fad"? Why did it take until 1947 for a black player to be permitted to play in the major leagues?

That's why.

Eddie Mathews.

In an era of particularly heavy hitting in the National League, Milwaukee's Eddie Mathews was one of the prime rocket launchers. The power-hitting third baseman was one of the most consistent home run hitters who ever lived, a fact borne out by the National League record he holds—nine consecutive years (1953–1961) of 30 or more home runs. Eddie served notice early when he became the first National League rookie ever to hit 3 home runs in a game (against the Dodgers at Ebbets Field on September 27, 1952).

Mathews holds the distinction of having played with the Braves in all three of their ports of call—Boston, Milwaukee, and Atlanta, serving just one year each in Boston and Atlanta.

Eddie was born in Texarkana, Texas, on October 13, 1931. His distance hitting in high school attracted attention, to the extent that on the night of his graduation 15 of the 16 big-league clubs had scouts in attendance, each clutching a contract and a checkbook. Still wearing the tuxedo he had graduated in, the seventeen-year-old signed with the Braves and began the long, dynamite-laden career that would culminate with his election to the Hall of Fame in 1978.

Eddie hit 40 or more home runs four times, with a high of 47 in 1953, his second year in the majors. He also drove in over 100 runs five times, with 135 in 1953 his best.

Ironically, in light of all his slugging (which included a game-winning tenth-inning home run against the Yankees in the fourth game of the 1957 World Series), Eddie's most memorable moment on a ball field occurred with a glove on his hand. It took place in the seventh game of the 1957 Series against the Yankees at Yankee Stadium. It was the bottom of the ninth, the Braves were winning 5–0, there were two out, the bases were loaded, and Bill Skowron was at bat. A base hit would bring the tying run to the plate. Skowron lashed a low scorching shot down the line; Mathews broke to his right, gloved the ball, and leaped jubilantly on the bag to give Milwaukee the championship.

Mathews was a durable player, and a rugged one. He was known as a bruising adversary in on-the-field brawls, and in fact one of his managers once commented that had he not gone in for baseball, Mathews might well have been a heavyweight contender.

Eddie finished his career in 1968 playing for Detroit, where he hit the last of his 512 major-league home runs. He went out a winner, seeing brief service for the Tigers in the 1968 World Series.

Mathews returned to Atlanta in August 1972 as manager of the Braves, a job he held until July 21, 1974.

Jackie Robinson.

Pee Wee Reese.

Roy Campanella roaring safely home in a cloud of Ebbets Field dust, beating the tag of Cardinals catcher Bill Sarni. The action occurred on August 29, 1955.

Yogi Berra, a third MVP trophy in 1955.

Yankee rookie Elston Howard, who broke in as an outfielder in 1955, batting .290.

The Yankees' hard-throwing Tommy Byrne, 16–5 in 1955.

Detroit's twenty-year-old batting champion, Al Kaline.

Detroit's Ray Boone, co-RBI leader (with Jackie Jensen) in 1955.

Harry Agganis.

Brooklyn third baseman Don Hoak in levitation at Ebbets Field on May 30, 1955. That's Pittsburgh's Jerry Lynch taking third base safely on a wild pitch as Hoak dives for Roy Campanella's throw. Jocko Conlan is the umpire.

Eighteen-year-old Brooks Robinson in 1955.

Herb Score.

Ernie Banks.

Don Newcombe about to let 'er rip.

Dodger skipper Walter Alston congratulating pitcher Roger Craig after a winning effort. Note the size of Craig's hand.

Brooklyn's strong 1955 bullpen brigade. *Left to right:* Ed Roebuck, Don Bessent, and Clem Labine.

Johnny Podres, Brooklyn's World Series hero, who beat the Yankees in the seventh game of the 1955 Series.

Don Hoak, Brooklyn's backup third baseman.

Dodger outfielder Sandy Amoros, whose spectacular running catch in the seventh game was instrumental in Brooklyn's World Series victory.

Former National League home run king Ralph Kiner, who wound up his career with the Cleveland Indians in 1955. Forced out by a bad back at the age of thirty-two, Ralph hit 18 homers in his final year.

President Eisenhower getting the season under way on opening day in Washington. Immediately to Ike's left are Washington club owner Clark Griffith, Washington manager Charley Dressen, and Baltimore manager Paul Richards.

Red Sox outfielder Gene Stephens.

Right-hander Frank Sullivan, the Red Sox' 18-game winner in 1955.

Willard Nixon, who pitched for the Red Sox throughout the 1950s.

A clutch of Red Sox infielders smiling in the Fenway sunshine. *Left to right:* Ted Lepcio, Eddie Joost, Billy Goodman, Norm Zauchin. Zauchin hit 27 home runs in 1955.

Cincinnati's Ted Kluszewski sliding home safely against the Giants at the Polo Grounds. Giants catcher Ray Katt seems to be looking after an errant peg. Jocko Conlan is the umpire.

Don Zimmer, a utility infielder for the Dodgers in 1955.

Robin Roberts.

Solly Hemus, St. Louis Cardinals utility infielder.

Alex Grammas, playing short-stop for the Cardinals in 1955.

Stan Musial showing the bat with which he hit his three hundredth career home run during the 1955 season.

Wally Post, Cincinnati's free-swinging outfielder, who hit 40 home runs in 1955 and batted .309.

New York Giants southpaw Don Liddle, 10–4 in 1955.

Stan Musial, whose home run won the 1955 All-Star Game for the National League, showing off his bat to pitchers Gene Conley *(left)* of Milwaukee and southpaw Joe Nuxhall of the Reds. Joe won 17 that year.

Chicago White Sox left-hander Jack Harshman. He came to the big leagues in the late 1940s as a first baseman with the New York Giants, who later dealt him to the White Sox, where he was converted into a winning pitcher.

Red Sox relief pitcher Leo Kiely.

The Amoros catch in the sixth inning of the seventh game of the 1955 World Series. Sandy had to come a long way for it. "He never worried about running into the fence," said Walter Alston. "That was the key thing."

Brooklyn's Don Newcombe, 27–7 in 1956.

1·9·5·6

In 1956, three National League teams locked elbows and put on one of the most gripping pennant races in major-league history, a race that wasn't settled until the final day of the season. It was the fourth time in seven years that the champagne had to remain corked until the last out of the last game, and for the fourth time one of the clubs involved was the Brooklyn Dodgers, a team that seemed to have a penchant for driving its fans to the furthest extremities of tension.

The race featured Walter Alston's world-champion Dodgers, aging now but still formidable; Fred Haney's hard-hitting Milwaukee Braves; and Birdie Tebbetts's even harder-hitting Cincinnati Reds, who that year tied the record of the 1947 Giants by hitting 221 home runs.

The Braves led from the start of the season until early June, slumped a bit that month, came back with a 42–14 record in July and August, but then slipped to 14–13 in September, and the slip was fatal.

The Dodgers played steadily rather than spectacularly, never more than a handful of games behind. The Reds, who were in first place briefly in June and mid-July, never seemed quite able to make the dramatic surge that would have driven them past the Dodgers and Braves.

Going into the season's final weekend, the Braves held a one-game lead over the Dodgers and two over the Reds. On Friday night the Braves and Reds lost, while the Dodgers were rained out. On Saturday the Braves and Reds lost again, while the Dodgers were sweeping a doubleheader from the Pirates. The day's work eliminated the Reds and left the Dodgers in first place by one game with one to play.

Knowing that a victory would give them their second straight pennant and fourth in five years, irrespective of what the Braves did, the Dodgers went to work against the Pirates immediately. A three-run homer by Duke Snider in the first inning sent them off to a lusty start; Snider later hit another home run, Sandy Amoros hit two, and the Dodgers won 8–6, assuring their ninth and final Brooklyn pennant.

Despite some slippage on the part of a few of their veterans, there was still enough firepower left in Brooklyn. Just enough. Roy Campanella had a wretched season, batting .219 with 20 home runs; the thirty-seven-year-old Pee Wee Reese batted .257, the thirty-seven-year-old Jackie Robinson .275. But Duke Snider had another premier year, leading the league with 43 home runs, while Gil Hodges hit 32. Jim Gilliam, batting .300 on the button, was the only Dodger to bat that high.

On the mound for Brooklyn it was all Don Newcombe. The big right-hander followed up his 20–5 year with a gaudy 27–7 record, winning more than any other two Dodger pitchers combined. Carl Erskine slipped to 13–11, but on May 12 the stylish right-hander came up with his second no-hitter, muffling the Giants at Ebbets Field.

Early in the season it was evident the Dodgers needed one more starter (World Series hero Johnny Podres had gone into the Navy). After trying unsuccessfully to make a trade, they began scanning the waiver lists and came up with one of the most unlikely names possible. The name was Sal Maglie, ex–Giant ace, ex–Dodger killer, and probably the most disliked (by Dodger fans) of all New York Giant players. Waived to Cleveland the year before, Maglie was sitting on the Indian bench, unable to crack Al Lopez's formidable starting rotation. "Take him," Cleveland general manager Hank Greenberg told Dodger vice-president Buzzy Bavasi. "He's still a hell of a guy."

Bavasi took the gamble, and it proved a most fortunate one, for without Maglie there would have been no pennant for Brooklyn that year. The club's erstwhile nemesis arrived on May 15

1·9·5·6

and went to work compiling a 13–5 record that included a no-hitter against the Phillies on September 25, at the very peak of the pennant race.

The second-place Braves, hitting 177 homers to Brooklyn's 179, saw young Henry Aaron emerge as a first-rank star that year. The twenty-two-year-old Alabaman hit 26 home runs and led the league with a .328 batting average, 200 hits, and 34 doubles. Joe Adcock banged 38 homers, Eddie Mathews 37, and ex-Giant Bobby Thomson 20.

Warren Spahn was again Milwaukee's ace with a 20–11 record, followed by Lew Burdette's 19–11 and Bob Buhl's 18–8, with Burdette leading the league with six shutouts and a 2.71 ERA. Buhl, a rugged right-hander, gave the Dodgers fits all year, beating them in eight of nine decisions. Not since Grover Cleveland Alexander beat the Reds eight times in 1916 had a major-league pitcher enjoyed such success against a single club. (The record of nine was set by Chicago's Ed Reulbach against the Dodgers in 1908.) For Buhl to register so many decisions against a single club was unusual but hardly extraordinary; in those years of the eight-club league and 154-game schedule, teams played each other 22 times in eight separate series.

After 11 straight second-division finishes, the Cincinnati Reds finally came charging into the first division and nearly won a pennant doing it. Birdie Tebbetts's men did it mainly with brawn. To an already powerhouse attack that included Ted Kluszewski, Wally Post, and Gus Bell, the club added catcher Ed Bailey and an awesome new young talent, twenty-year-old outfielder Frank Robinson, the league's first unanimous choice for Rookie of the Year. Robinson, destined to become a Triple Crown winner, the only man ever to win MVP honors in both leagues, the first black to manage in the major leagues, and a Hall of Famer, broke in with a

powerful year. His 38 home runs tied Wally Berger's 1930 record for a rookie, while he batted .290 and drove in 83 runs.

Kluszewski hit 35 home runs, Post 36, Bell 29, and Bailey 28. With a slick double-play combination of Roy McMillan at short and Johnny Temple at second, the Reds were a solid team. On August 18, they exploded with a record-tying eight home runs against the Braves on their way to a 13–4 win. Leading the barrage was reserve outfielder Bob Thurman with three homers, followed by Kluszewski and Robinson with two apiece and Post with one. The eight home runs tied a single-game record established by the 1939 Yankees and equaled by the 1953 Braves. With two homers of their own, the Braves made it a two-team total of ten, which tied the National League record.

What kept the Cincinnati steamroller from the pennant was baseball's most chronic complaint—not enough pitching. Right-hander Brooks Lawrence, winner of his first 13 decisions, was the ace with a 19–10 record. No other Red starter won more than 13.

With nine National Leaguers swatting over 30 home runs, the runs-batted-in title was won with a remarkably low total—the lowest, in fact, since 1920. Stan Musial, who hit 27 homers, was the RBI leader with 109.

For Philadelphia's Robin Roberts, it was the first time since 1949 that he failed to post the magic "20" in the win column, though the great Phillie right-hander came as close as possible with a 19–18 record. Hitters around the league were saying that some of the dash had gone out of Roberts's low, sizzling fast ball, the consequence of six straight years of delivering over 300 innings of work. And in fact, Roberts's 20-game-winning seasons were over. Though he would spend another decade in the big leagues, no longer would he be the dominant pitcher he once was.

The only other National League pitcher to

1·9·5·6

join Newcombe and Spahn in the pitchers' "magic circle" was New York's Johnny Antonelli, who turned in a 20–13 record. Antonelli's teammate Willie Mays saw his home run production drop from 51 to a still respectable 36; but Willie added yet another color to his stylish palette when he led the league with 40 stolen bases, highest in the league since Kiki Cuyler's 43 in 1929.

Two members of the seventh-place Pittsburgh Pirates turned in record-setting performances in 1956. First baseman Dale Long put on a game-by-game home run streak that finally outdid anything ever achieved by Ruth, Foxx, Kiner, Greenberg, or anyone else. For eight consecutive games, between May 19 and May 28, Long hit one homer per game, setting a new record (the previous record was six, shared by five players: Ken Williams in 1922, George Kelly in 1924, Lou Gehrig in 1931, Walker Cooper in 1947, and Willie Mays in 1955). Long was stopped by Don Newcombe on May 29.

Pirate relief pitcher Roy Face established his own all-time record when he pitched in nine consecutive games between September 3 and September 13, breaking the major-league record of eight straight appearances set by Ben Flowers of the Red Sox and Hoyt Wilhelm of the Giants, both in 1953. (The record has since been broken by Mike Marshall of the Los Angeles Dodgers, who appeared in thirteen straight games in 1974.)

There was a newly created postseason award that year, the Cy Young Award for baseball's top pitcher. As originally instituted, this prestigious designation was given to a single pitcher. Beginning in 1967, it was administered in a format similar to that of the Most Valuable Player—one in each league. The first Cy Young Award was given to Brooklyn's Don Newcombe; and with the big right-hander also winning the Most Valuable Player trophy that year,

it gave Newk a rare clean sweep.

On December 13, an era came to a close in Brooklyn. On that date the Dodgers traded Jackie Robinson to the Giants for left-hander Dick Littlefield and cash estimated at $35,000. Robinson, however, now thirty-seven years old, had already secretly planned his retirement, the story of which he had sold to a national magazine. When the story broke, the deal was nullified and the Brooklyn executive suite seethed. But that was Robinson, never bland, never orthodox. The episode gave Jackie a last laugh over an employer (Walter O'Malley) whom he had never particularly liked anyway.

In the American League it was the year of Mickey Mantle, the year when Mantle, whose rise to greatness had been forecast and anticipated since 1951, crested and performed at flood tide all summer.

Mickey had come along year by year steadily but unspectacularly, that dazzling talent always right at the surface, always threateningly imminent, sometimes ripping free, as with his 565-foot home run in 1953. In 1955 there were indications that the last shades of "potential" had risen and gone forever, when he led the league with 37 home runs and a .611 slugging percentage.

And then, in 1956, Mantle soared to greatness as he unleashed the most sustained and power-laden attack of the postwar years. The twenty-four-year-old Yankee center fielder became only the sixth American League hitter to win a Triple Crown when he led the league with a .353 batting average, 52 home runs, and 130 runs batted in. (The previous Triple Crown winners were a sublime crew indeed: Nap Lajoie, Ty Cobb, Jimmie Foxx, Lou Gehrig, and Ted Williams, who did it twice and missed a third by a flea's eyelash.)

As added seasoning, Mantle was throughout the summer a distinct threat to baseball's most

1·9·5·6

glamorous single-season record—Ruth's 60 homers in 1927. Entering the September doorway, Mickey had 47 homers, 4 ahead of Ruth's 1927 pace. Mantle, however, swatted just 5 more in September. When he hit his fiftieth, the Oklahoma power plant joined another select list of crescendo names: Ruth, Foxx, and Greenberg—the only other American Leaguers to hit as many home runs in a season.

Led by Mantle, the Yankees rolled to their easiest pennant under Stengel, giving the wily old manipulator seven top-rung finishes in eight years, matching what Joe McCarthy's Yankees had done from 1936 to 1943.

The Yankees hit 190 home runs, with Berra (30), Bauer (26), and Skowron (23) helping Mantle deliver souvenirs to the paying customers. The 190 one-way tickets set a new American League record, exceeding the mark of 182 set by the 1936 Yankees.

Whitey Ford led the pitchers with a 19–6 record and the league's lowest earned-run average, 2.47. Stengel also received surprisingly strong seasons from young sinker-balling righthander Johnny Kucks (18–9) and righty Tom Sturdivant (16–8).

The Yankees took command in May with a 21–10 record, played well in June, and then ran away from the pack in July when they won 23 of 29, going on to finish nine games ahead of their perennial pursuers, Al Lopez and his Cleveland Indians.

For the six seasons from 1950 through 1955, Cleveland had ten 20-game winners, and in 1956 they had three more: Bob Lemon (20–14), Early Wynn (20–9), and the sensational young Herb Score (20–9). Ted Williams had described Score as the most scintillating southpaw he had ever seen, and in 1956 the young fireballer bore out the encomium of baseball's greatest and most astute batsman. In his second season, Score led in strikeouts with 263 (no other big-league pitcher had as many

as 200 that year) and shutouts with 5.

The other member of Cleveland's starting rotation, Mike Garcia, dropped to 11–12. This was indeed a "Big Four" that Lopez ran through the league that year—combined, Lemon, Wynn, Score, and Garcia started 133 of Cleveland's 154 games.

Slowing the track for the Indians was a .244 team batting average, lowest in the league and 26 points under the first-place Yankees. Their top hitter was first baseman Vic Wertz, with 32 home runs and 106 runs batted in. Wertz was the second-highest home run hitter in the league with his 32—20 behind Mantle. It was the biggest disparity between the two top American League home run hitters since 1928, when Ruth hit 54 to Gehrig's runner-up 27.

The Indians made a notable addition to their lineup in outfielder Rocky Colavito, soon to become one of the league's loudest guns. The twenty-two-year-old rookie broke in with 21 home runs and brought caution to the base paths with a cannonlike throwing arm in right field.

Another brilliant new young talent entered the American League that year. He was Luis Aparicio, twenty-two-year-old shortstop for the White Sox, a future Hall of Famer who was considered one of the greatest defensive shortstops of all time. The league's Rookie of the Year for 1956, Aparicio batted .266 and led with 21 stolen bases, the first of nine consecutive years he was to top the league in that still-neglected department.

Also shining for the White Sox in 1956 were lefty Billy Pierce with a 20–9 record and outfielder Minnie Minoso, who batted .316.

The Boston Red Sox seemed to have taken out a lease on fourth place, finishing in the slot for the fourth straight year. As usual, the Bosox sent up a solid hitting attack, and, as usual, they were undermined by mixed performances on the mound. Only rookie right-hander Tom

1·9·5·6

Brewer won big, with a 19–9 record. Boston's nominal ace, left-hander Mel Parnell, who was bothered by injuries all year, nevertheless fired up the league's only no-hitter. It came against the White Sox at Fenway Park on July 14 and was the first no-hitter thrown by a Red Sox pitcher since 1923 and the first ever at Fenway by a left-hander, the park being a notorious graveyard for southpaws.

The Red Sox had three former batting titlists in the lineup—Mickey Vernon, Billy Goodman, and Ted Williams. The veteran Vernon batted .310, Goodman .293, and Williams .345. In addition, Jackie Jensen batted .315 and drove in 97 runs.

On July 17, Williams became only the fifth major leaguer to hit 400 home runs. Ahead of him on the long-ball list at the time were Ruth with 714; Foxx, 534; Mel Ott, 511; and Gehrig, 493. (By the end of the 1985 season, there were 21 players with over 400 lifetime homers.)

On August 7, Williams, never the bashful type, was memorably exasperated in a game at Fenway Park. When he found himself the object of booing after muffing a fly ball, the irritated Theodore started spraying saliva as he trotted to the dugout after the inning. He entered the dugout, then bounced out again and let fly another wet response to his detractors. Red Sox owner Tom Yawkey was so offended by his star's behavior that he slammed Teddy with a $5,000 fine. The following night, Ted belted a titanic home run. After spinning around the bases, the slugger whimsically clamped his hand over his mouth as he ducked into the dugout, with the crowd roaring in appreciation.

Reportedly, Yawkey never deducted the fine from Ted's paycheck.

For Detroit, it was a season of frustration. The Tigers had two 20-game winners, four .300 hitters, a league-high .279 team batting average—and a fifth-place finish.

Tiger right-hander Frank Lary was 21–13, while southpaw Billy Hoeft was 20–14. Righty Paul Foytack was 15–13, but no other Tiger pitcher won more than 8.

Young Al Kaline proved that his batting crown of the year before was no fluke, following it up with another solid season, batting .314, hitting 27 home runs, and driving in 128 runs, just two fewer than Mantle. Harvey Kuenn batted .332 and for the third time in four years rapped out the most hits, 196. Outfielder Charlie Maxwell batted .326 and hit 28 home runs. Charlie had the curious habit of belting homers on Sundays, when crowds were largest, and consequently became enormously popular in Detroit. Detroit's other .300 sticker was third baseman Ray Boone, checking in at .308.

Meeting in the World Series for the sixth time in ten years, the Dodgers and Yankees put on a rousing seven-game Series won by the Yankees. The Series was marked by the greatest individual pitching effort ever seen in postseason play. In Game 5, the Yankees' Don Larsen, an 11–5 pitcher during the season who had been knocked out of the box in the second inning of the second game, made baseball history. Using a novel no-windup delivery, the big right-hander saw 27 Dodger hitters and retired them all in order, pitching a perfect no-hit, no-run game against one of baseball's strongest lineups.

For Stengel, it was his sixth World Series victory (over an eight-year span), leaving him one behind Joe McCarthy's managerial record of seven.

Mickey Mantle, Triple Crown winner.

Mickey Mantle

Superlatives followed Mickey Mantle throughout his baseball career. Tom Greenwade, the Yankee scout who signed Mickey in 1949, told his bosses that the youngster had a chance to be "a great ballplayer." Credit Greenwade for knowing his business.

After batting .313 and .383 in the low minors, Mickey was invited to the Yankees' spring training camp in 1951. It was supposed to be strictly a look-see for Casey Stengel and the Yankee brass. Mickey was penciled in to play Class A ball at Binghamton, New York, that year. A few weeks later, they decided the kid was too good for Class A and they would send him instead to Kansas City, then a Yankee Triple-A club in the American Association.

But Mickey continued to hit 500-foot blasts in spring training and outrun every player in camp—by such margins that the first time the Yankees saw him race they asked him to do it over again, convinced that the others must have stumbled getting away.

Mickey dazzled throughout spring training, hitting well over .400 in exhibition games, until Stengel, after 40 years in baseball, had to admit that he had never seen anything like the young Oklahoman, particularly Mickey's ability to pulverize a pitched ball from either side of the plate.

Mantle was born in Spavinaw, Oklahoma, on October 20, 1931. As a boy he was taught baseball most studiously by his father, who had programmed his firstborn to be a big-league player. Mickey thrived on all sports, baseball in particular. His batting feats finally attracted the attention of Greenwade, who signed him for a bonus of $1,100.

Forgetting Binghamton and then Kansas City in that spring of 1951, the Yankees brought Mickey to New York with them and he opened the season in right field, with Joe DiMaggio (whom Mickey was being groomed to replace) in center. A batting slump in July sent him to Kansas City for a month, but he was back in August, to stay.

Injuries were the bane of Mantle's career, and they were frequent, numerous, and often serious. Despite playing much of his career bandaged and in pain, he went on to become one of the great power hitters in baseball history, and one of the most feared, leading the league in walks five times. "They just didn't want to pitch to him," longtime American League manager Paul Richards said. "That's all there was to it. He was too strong, too awesome."

His Triple Crown season in 1956 put the seal on Mantle's greatness. He batted over .300 nine times. He led in home runs four times, slugging percentage four times, total bases three times, and runs scored six times—that last figure being topped in baseball history only by Ruth, who led eight times.

Mantle hit 536 home runs lifetime, and holds the World Series record with 18 homers.

Whitey Ford, 19–6 in '956.

Don Larsen, 11–5 for the Yankees in 1956, with the big one coming up in October.

Frank Robinson.

The Yankees' Tom Sturdivant, 16–8 in 1956. *(Photo by Bob Olen.)*

Frank Lary, Detroit's fine 20-game-winning right-hander.

Left-hander Billy Hoeft, who was 20–14 in 1956. It was the Tiger pitcher's best year in the big leagues.

Two titans getting together in spring training. That's Stan Musial on the left, and Ted Williams. Somebody had just asked them if hitting a baseball was difficult.

Four seasoned members of the Brooklyn Lumber Company. *Left to right:* Gil Hodges, Roy Campanella, Duke Snider, Carl Furillo.

Smoky Burgess, a sharp-hitting catcher who played for the Phillies, Reds, and Pirates in the 1950s. *(Courtesy of the Cincinnati Reds.)*

Nobody, but nobody, could run them down in the outfield better than the Red Sox' intense, colorful Jimmy Piersall.

The Chicago White Sox' superb left-hander, Billy Pierce. He was 20–9 in 1956.

Fast baller Tom Brewer won 19 for the Red Sox in 1956.

Luis Aparicio of the Chicago White Sox, who set the standard at shortstop.

The Cardinals' Ken Boyer, one of baseball's great third basemen.

Cincinnati's hard-hitting catcher, Ed Bailey, who hit 28 home runs in 1956.

Another long-balling National League catcher, Stan Lopata of the Phillies, who hit 32 home runs in 1956.

Detroit catcher Frank House.

Mickey Mantle, shouldering three bats and holding up three fingers symbolic of his Triple Crown season in 1956. *(Photo by Bob Olen.)*

Big Jim Lemon. The Washington outfielder had 27 homers in 1956.

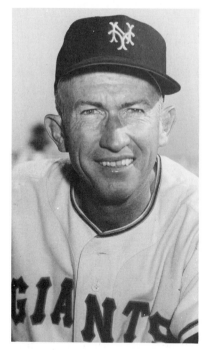

Former Giants infielder Bill Rigney, who replaced Leo Durocher as Giants manager in 1956.

Pirate first baseman Dale Long has just set a new major-league record by homering in seven consecutive games. The jubilant gentleman with him is manager Bobby Bragan. The next day, Long extended his own record to eight straight games, before being stopped.

Alvin Dark, for a decade one of the National League's top shortstops. Coming up with the Braves in 1948, he later played for the Giants, Cardinals, Cubs, and Phillies. Dark then had a second career as a manager, heading the Giants, Athletics, Indians, Athletics again, and Padres.

Milwaukee right-hander Ray Crone.

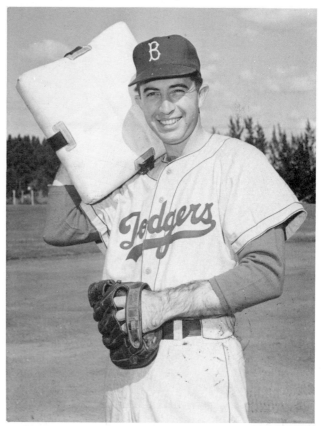

Carl Erskine in action.

Dodger third baseman Randy Jackson stole very few bases. This seems to be one of them.

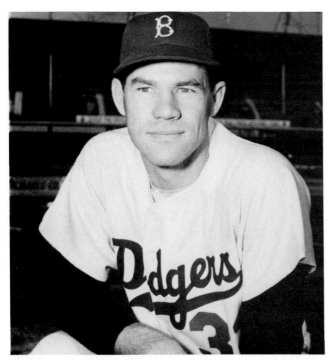

Backup first baseman Rocky Nelson, who played for the Dodgers and Cardinals in 1956.

Brooklyn's Sal Maglie has just pitched a no-hitter against the Phillies at Ebbets Field on September 25, 1956, and in a burst of enthusiastic generosity team president Walter O'Malley is giving Sal a handshake and a $500 bonus (note those greenbacks).

Eddie Yost, sharp-eyed third baseman of the Washington Senators. They called him "the Walking Man," for his ability to coax bases on balls out of pitchers. In 1956, he drew 151 walks. Only Ruth and Williams have drawn more in a season.

Charlie Silvera, year after year backup man to Yogi Berra, which meant he seldom got to play.

Some of the bigger noisemakers in the Pittsburgh Pirate lineup in 1956. *Left to right:* Roberto Clemente, Frank Thomas, Lee Walls, and Bill Virdon.

At bat, Ted Williams.

St. Louis Cardinal right-hander Tom Poholsky.

Veteran outfielder Ron Northey. In 1956, playing for the White Sox, he was the American League's top pinch hitter.

Dave Sisler, Boston Red Sox right-hander. He was the brother of Dick Sisler and son of Hall of Fame first baseman George Sisler.

That's Brooklyn's Jackie Robinson—thirty-seven years old or not—stealing home against the Giants at Ebbets Field on April 25, 1956. Catcher Wes Westrum is lunging for the elusive target, while Charley Neal and umpire Stan Landes bear witness.

Ike Delock (left) and Jimmy Piersall.

Detroit right-hander Paul Foytack, one of the American League's hardest throwers.

Mickey Mantle taking a big rip in the 1956 World Series. Roy Campanella is the catcher.

Don Larsen delivering the ninety-seventh and final pitch of his perfect game against the Dodgers in the fifth game of the 1956 World Series. That's second baseman Billy Martin in the background.

A night game in Ebbets Field in August 1957. Those empty seats spelled a move to Los Angeles in 1958.

1·9·5·7

Looking back, it seems to have been inevitable, maybe even logical; but at the time people found it stunning and incredible. Some called it an outrage and an unconscionable betrayal. It was the most unadorned demonstration of the baseball-is-a-business reality that fans had ever received.

For the first time since 1882, New York was going to be without National League representation, as not one but both of the city's senior circuit teams heeded America's oldest siren call and headed west. The 50 years of stability that had been broken with the Boston Braves' move to Milwaukee in 1953, followed by the St. Louis Browns going to Baltimore and the Philadelphia Athletics to Kansas City, now saw the most startling migrations of all—the Brooklyn Dodgers to Los Angeles and the New York Giants to San Francisco.

The Giants, suffering from declining attendance and an increasingly blighted area around the Polo Grounds, were more aboveboard about their intentions. In July, owner Horace Stoneham announced that he would recommend to his board of directors that the club be moved (it was said that their original destination was to be Minneapolis, where the Giants operated their top farm club), and on August 19 it became official—the Giants were leaving, to relocate in San Francisco.

Walter O'Malley did not announce his club's move to Los Angeles until after the season, but the indications had been there for several years. O'Malley had said in 1955 that the Dodgers hoped to leave Ebbets Field by 1958. (At that time, the Dodger president was still hoping the city would build a municipally owned stadium for his club, but this never materialized.) In February 1957, the Dodgers bought the Chicago Cubs' Pacific Coast League franchise in Los Angeles. In March, Los Angeles mayor Norris Poulsen turned up at Brooklyn's spring training camp at Vero Beach, Florida, to confer with O'Malley. By that time, O'Malley was probably singing "California, Here I Come" in the shower.

On September 16, the city of Los Angeles made the Dodger boss a most sumptuous offer—the transfer of some 307 acres of city-owned land in an undeveloped area called Chavez Ravine, less than ten minutes from downtown Los Angeles. For this the Dodgers would pay $4,400,000. The city would obligate itself to spend a few million to grade the site and the county another few million to build connecting roads and freeways to facilitate access to the ball park to be built at Chavez Ravine. Until the new stadium could be raised, the Dodgers would play their games in the city's enormous Memorial Coliseum, an arena built for almost any athletic activity but baseball. But the Coliseum's bizarre configurations (there would have to be a comically short left field and ludicrously distant center and right fields) were negated—in O'Malley's mind—by a 100,000 seating capacity.

O'Malley faced some roadblocks along the journey to the end of the rainbow. A lot of people were offended by the largesse the city was begging the Dodger owner to accept. The transaction was taken to a referendum the following year, which the Dodgers won (by a surprisingly narrow margin).

Horace Stoneham in San Francisco had a smoother journey. While the Giants were playing in tiny Seals Stadium, the city built the team a brand-new stadium. The only problem turned out to be the location, Candlestick Point, an elbow of land jutting into the bay. When the Giants finally moved into their new home, they realized that a serious mistake had been made. Strong swirling winds came pouring in off the bay in late afternoon, playing havoc with fly balls, chilling the nights, and making Candlestick Park a most uncomfortable place to play or watch baseball in.

1·9·5·7

With all the turmoil surrounding them that season, neither the Dodgers nor the Giants worked themselves into the pennant race. The Dodgers, seeking a third straight pennant, were derailed by the decline of some of their aging stars and by faltering pitching; but more than that, it was the solid hitting and strong pitching of the Milwaukee Braves that finally put an end to the eastern division's dominance, the Braves becoming the first western club to take the National League pennant since the 1946 St. Louis Cardinals.

Leading the Braves on offense was Henry Aaron, getting better each year. The young outfielder slammed a league-high 44 home runs, drove in a league-high 132 runs, and batted .322. Eddie Mathews hit 32 homers. Rounding out an inordinately well-balanced lineup were veteran second baseman Red Schoendienst (acquired from the Giants in a mid-season trade), first baseman Frank Torre, shortstop Johnny Logan, catcher Del Crandall, and outfielders Billy Bruton and Wes Covington. The Braves even had a player who carved out a modest legend for himself. He was Bob Hazle, rushed into the lineup when the Braves suffered some late-season injuries in the outfield. Hazle got into 41 games, hit 7 home runs, and batted .403. He became known as "Hurricane Hazle." But his success and his celebrity were brief; before the next season was out he was gone.

Milwaukee starting pitching was the strongest in the league. Warren Spahn was a 20-game winner for the eighth time, with a 21–11 record, followed by Bob Buhl's 18–7 and Lew Burdette's 17–9. Manager Fred Haney's Big Three remained in charge throughout the year, pitching the Braves to a comfortable eight-game lead over the second-place Cardinals. Spahn's excellent season (he was the league's only 20-game winner that year) earned him the second Cy Young Award.

For Stan Musial, the year brought a rejuvenation. After winning six batting titles in nine years, the Cardinal icon had seen four years go by and the titles going to other hitters; in addition, his batting averages were quietly going down, to .310 in 1956, the lowest of his career. While most hitters would have dined out all winter on .310, for Stan Musial it was distressing. In 1957, however, he came roaring back with a superb .351 average, good enough to take his seventh and final batting crown, embellishing it with 29 home runs and 102 runs batted in.

Along with Musial, the Cardinals rolled out one of the league's better lineups (they had the best team batting average, with a .274 mark), including Ken Boyer, Alvin Dark, Del Ennis, Wally Moon, and utility man Joe Cunningham, who batted .318. Pitching was the culprit in St. Louis, with only right-handers Larry Jackson and Lindy McDaniel winning as high as 15.

Walter Alston's club dropped to third, 11 games out, a team clearly in a state of transition, and not just from Brooklyn to Los Angeles. Jackie Robinson was retired, Pee Wee Reese was thirty-eight years old (a fact reflected in his .224 batting average), and Roy Campanella hit just 13 home runs and batted .242. Duke Snider, though slipping to a .274 batting average, did hit 40 home runs for the fifth year in a row, tying him with Ralph Kiner as the only National Leaguers ever to attain the 40–home run level for that many consecutive years.

With Don Newcombe dropping to a lackluster 11–12 record and Carl Erskine all but useless with a sore arm, the only bright note on the Brooklyn mound that year was sophomore right-hander Don Drysdale. The twenty-year-old sidewheeler ran up a 17–9 record in the first burst of the greatness that would keep adding cylinders in Los Angeles. Though left-hander Johnny Podres led the league with six shutouts and a 2.66 earned-run average, his record was just 12–9. Sal Maglie, Brooklyn's Cinderella man of a year ago, dropped to 6–6 and was released before the season ended.

1·9·5·7

Cincinnati continued depositing baseballs over walls, with four men hitting 20 or more: George Crowe (31), Frank Robinson (29), and Wally Post and Ed Bailey (20 each). Robinson followed up his great rookie season with those 29 homers and a .322 batting average. Crowe broke into the lineup as a first-base replacement for Ted Kluszewski, who sat out much of the year with a back injury.

The Phillies had the Rookie of the Year in right-hander Jack Sanford (at twenty-eight a fairly ripe rookie), who stormed the league with a 19–8 record and the most strikeouts (188).

Though outshone by Most Valuable Player Henry Aaron, Willie Mays continued to be just about sensational in the now-doomed Polo Grounds. Willie batted .333, hitting 35 home runs and a league-leading 20 triples. Showing his extraordinary versatility, he also led in stolen bases again, with 38. "Is there anything he can't do?" a writer asked one of Willie's Giant teammates. "Yeah," came the reply. "He can't carry a tune too well."

Chicago's Ernie Banks, warming up for what were going to be two straight Most Valuable Player awards, belted 43 home runs and drove across 102 runs.

Milwaukee fans gave success a good name, coming out in record numbers to watch their team win a pennant. When the last turnstile had clicked, Milwaukee had set a new National League attendance record with 2,215,404.

The most remarkable occurrence in the American League in 1957 was not the New York Yankees winning their eighth pennant in nine years, though that was no small achievement. But in baseball, the moment is more dramatic than the man and the man more compelling than the team, and in 1957 the most enthralling spectacle involved a single gifted player dramatically manifesting in spectacular enlargement what was perhaps the ultimate peak of his unique abilities. The player was Ted

Williams, a man who already had more badges and decorations than a field marshal.

How does a .400 hitter surpass himself? Well, the best he can do is approach his own standard, but if he is thirty-nine years old when he does it, then he has in a very real sense outdone himself. Swinging with robust consistency all season, Williams batted a rarefied .388, baseball's highest batting average since Ted's own .406 in 1941. And this was a lethal .388, a rock-hard .388, with 38 home runs (one for every 11 official times at bat) and a .731 slugging average (a figure surpassed in American League history only by Ruth and Foxx). With the thirty-six-year-old Stan Musial leading the National League, it was a banner year for baseball's version of the senior citizen.

A year before, Mantle had outhit Williams, .353 to .345. In 1957, Mantle attained his personal peak of .365 and wasn't even close to the top. It was as though the old master had decided to give the younger man a chastising lecture on presumption.

Two years previously, Al Kaline had become the youngest player ever to win a batting crown. Now it was Ted Williams setting a new standard at the other end of the chronological pole.

The other most dramatic individual story of the year in the American League was a downright tragic one.

In the spring, Boston's Tom Yawkey, stuffed with money from his ears to his shoes, had made the Cleveland Indians an outright cash offer of $1,000,000 for Herb Score. (This was when that sum of money was still a vapor for dreamers and not dispensed yearly to .260 hitters.) Though no doubt sorely tempted, the Indians did the seemly thing and turned the lucrative offer down. On the night of May 7, however, the Indians saw the career of their meteoric young left-hander come crashing, for all intents and purposes, to an end.

Score, who put a mighty effort into every pitch, an effort that twisted his body far to the

1·9·5·7

right and left him in an awkward—and defenseless—position after delivery, was working against the Yankees that night.

"I used to throw balls that I never saw reach the plate," Score said, "and when they were hit I had to look around to see where they were going. Very often I simply didn't see the ball after I'd let it go."

Well, he saw this pitch, after it was hit, but it was too late. The second batter of the game was Gil McDougald. Score delivered, fell out of position, heard the crack of the bat, and "I looked up and I can remember seeing the ball coming right into my eye. Boy, it had got big awfully fast and it was getting bigger. There was really nothing I could do about it. It hit me flush in the eye and as soon as it hit I remember saying to myself, 'Saint Jude, stay with me.' "

Score was fortunate—he did not lose his eye—but he was never the same pitcher again, and the rest of his aborted career consisted of comebacks, disabilities, and an occasional flash of the breathtaking talent that had been meant for the Hall of Fame.

Mickey Mantle's .365 batting average, though second best in the league, still earned him his second straight Most Valuable Player trophy. He hit 34 home runs and drove in 94 runs, figures reduced considerably by the 146 bases on balls he received. Pitchers, a breed with a survival instinct second to none, were becoming more and more disinclined to work on the Yankee strong man. How did you pitch to Mickey in a close game? "You didn't," said Cleveland's Mike Garcia.

Stengel's eighth pennant in nine shots was won by eight games over the White Sox, but it wasn't as easy as all that. On June 8, the Yankees were six games behind the surprising White Sox, now managed by Al Lopez. But on June 9, the Yankees launched a drive that gave them 26 wins in 32 games. On June 30, the Yankees moved into first place and never looked back.

Added to an already strong Yankee cast that included Mantle, Berra, Skowron, McDougald, Howard, and Bauer was Rookie of the Year Tony Kubek, a versatile twenty-year-old who batted .297 and played the outfield, shortstop, and third base with equal skill. "That's my kind of player," said an appreciative Stengel, who was a master of lineup juggling.

Making the club's 98 victories and pennant more notable was the fact that Tom Sturdivant was the big winner at 16–6, while Bob Turley won just 13, ERA leader (2.45) Bobby Shantz 11, and Whitey Ford, nagged by shoulder ailments, also 11.

Be it with Cleveland or now with Chicago, Al Lopez seemed destined to come in second. Managing the Indians, he was second in 1951, 1952, 1953, 1955, 1956, and again in 1957 with the White Sox. The Sox were short on power but long on singles and hustle. Nelson Fox batted .317 and Minnie Minoso .310, while Luis Aparicio remained dazzling at shortstop.

Pitching, always the hallmark of a Lopez team, was strong in Chicago that year. Billy Pierce was again the ace, the left-hander going 20–12, while righty Dick Donovan was 16–8 and Jim Wilson 15–8. White Sox right-hander Bob Keegan, 10–8 on the year, pitched the league's only no-hitter, muffling Washington on August 20.

The Red Sox broke out young third baseman Frank Malzone, who batted .292 and drove in 103 runs, the same number driven in by Jackie Jensen. It was Jensen, and not Mickey Mantle or Ted Williams or any other American League hitter, who was the league's leading run producer in the second half of the 1950s, averaging well over 100 RBIs a year between 1954 and 1959.

Detroit, expected to be a contender in 1957, suffered from off-seasons experienced by their star players. The batting averages of Harvey Kuenn and Al Kaline dipped below .300, while 1956's 20-game winners Frank Lary and Billy

1·9·5·7

Hoeft managed only 20 wins between them. The ace of the Tiger staff turned out to be right-hander Jim Bunning. The tall sidearmer launched what was to be a long and productive career with a strong 20–8 record, matching Billy Pierce for most wins.

Baltimore was breaking in a rangy young third baseman named Brooks Robinson. In the beginning there were some holes in the twenty-year-old's bat, though decidedly none in his glove. When Orioles manager Paul Richards was contemplating sending Robinson down to the minors to improve his hitting, Richards received a deputation. "The whole pitching staff came into my office," Richards said. "All of them. They heard I was thinking about sending Brooks down. They said they didn't care if Brooks never got a hit. They wanted him in there. That's how good he was with that glove."

With their once-formidable pitching starting to backslide now, the Cleveland Indians sank to sixth place. In addition to the injury to Score, Bob Lemon suffered elbow miseries and was reduced to a 6–11 record, while Mike Garcia had a modest 12–8 record and Early Wynn was 14–17.

For Washington Senators fans there wasn't much to cheer about except the smoking bat of outfielder Roy Sievers. Sievers became the first Washington hitter ever to lead the league in home runs, hitting a resounding 42, and only the second to lead in runs batted in, with 114 (Goose Goslin was the first, in 1924). The Washington club was apparently without a steal sign that year, establishing a new major-league low for thievery with just 13 stolen bases. Over their last 78 games they stole just 2 bases.

For the third straight year the World Series went to a full seven games. In the seventh game, Milwaukee's Lew Burdette made his third start of the Series. Working on just two days' rest, Burdette, a former Yankee farmhand, shut out Stengel's troops for the second time in pitching his third complete-game win, giving the Braves' franchise its first world championship since 1914. Burdette became the first pitcher to deliver three complete-game victories in a World Series since Stanley Coveleski did it for Cleveland against the Dodgers in 1920.

Ernie Banks.

Ernie Banks

The year 1931 was a fertile one for home run babies. No fewer than four robust little boys who each was to grow up to hit over 500 major-league home runs were born in that Depression year. Willie Mays came into the world on May 6, Eddie Mathews on October 13, Mickey Mantle on October 20, and the first of them, Ernie Banks, on January 31, in Dallas, Texas.

The tall, lean, right-handed ripper with the incredibly strong, quick wrists was playing for the Kansas City Monarchs—Jackie Robinson's old team—in the Negro League when the Chicago Cubs, looking for their first black player, spotted him. The Cubs thought enough of Ernie to pay the Monarchs $15,000 for him.

The Cubs decided that Ernie was ready for the big leagues, right now. The hard-hitting shortstop never played in the minors, one of a handful who started at the top and got better and better. In his first full season, 1954, Banks batted .275 and hit 19 home runs. Full-fledged stardom was just a year away—in 1955 he surprised everyone by hitting 44 home runs while driving in 117 runs and batting .295.

Five times between 1955 and 1960, Banks cleared the 40 mark in home runs, peaking with 47 in 1958, the year he won the first of his two straight Most Valuable Player awards. Swinging against powerful competition like Mays, Aaron, Snider, Kluszewski, and Mathews, Banks twice led in home runs and twice in runs batted in.

In 1955, Ernie set a major-league record (later tied by Jim Gentile of the Orioles in 1961) by hitting five grand slammers in a season.

His 47 home runs in 1958 gave Banks the all-time record for shortstops. In 1962, Banks, in deference to aching knees, switched over to first base, where his slugging seemed more appropriate.

Bad knees or not, Ernie was always a durable performer, playing in 150 or more games a season 12 times. Eight times in his career he drove in over 100 runs, the last time in 1969, when he was thirty-eight years old. That was the year the Cubs made a strong run for the pennant, only to fade in the stretch and be bypassed by the "Miracle Mets." It was the closest Ernie was to come to a World Series in his 19-year career.

Along with his hard and steady hitting, Banks endeared himself to Chicago fans through the congeniality of his disposition, to the extent that he was voted "Greatest Cub ever," and through the latter stages of his career was known as "Mr. Cub."

Banks retired after the 1971 season, leaving behind 512 home runs. He was voted into the Hall of Fame in 1977.

Milwaukee's rookie outfielder Hank Aaron.

Bill Bruton, Milwaukee center fielder and one of the fastest men in the National League.

Milwaukee right-hander Bob Buhl, 18–7 in 1957.

Milwaukee outfielder Andy Pafko, one of the most popular ballplayers of his time.

Johnny Logan, shortstop on Milwaukee's 1957 world champions.

Three Milwaukee pitchers going through the motions at Chicago's Wrigley Field. *Left to right:* Warren Spahn, Lew Burdette, and Gene Conley. They may look formidable, but there's not a single baseball among them.

Milwaukee's 1957 World Series hero, Lew Burdette.

Tony Kubek, the Yankees' versatile Rookie of the Year in 1957. *(Photo by Bob Olen.)*

Warren Spahn.

Mickey Mantle, a man of many skills.

Yankee southpaw Bobby Shantz, the American League's ERA leader in 1957.

Here's a rookie outfielder with Cleveland. His name is Roger Maris. He broke in with 14 home runs and a .235 batting average. He would do better a few years later.

Washington's Roy Sievers: 42 homers in 1957.

Stan Musial. In 1957 a .351 batting average and a seventh batting title.

Detroit's Jim Bunning, 20–8 in 1957.

Pittsburgh shortstop Dick Groat, a .315 hitter in 1957.

Bill Mazeroski of the Pittsburgh Pirates, as good a fielding second baseman as ever lived.

Cardinals right-hander Lindy McDaniel.

Larry Jackson, the Cardinals' curve-balling right-hander. He was 15–9 in 1957.

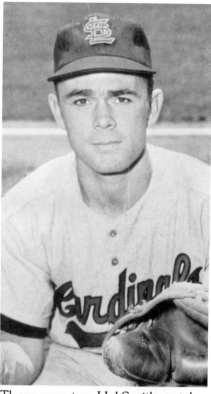

There were two Hal Smiths catching in the big leagues in the 1950s. This one was with the Cardinals.

Ed Bouchee, Phillies first baseman.

Cincinnati first baseman George Crowe, who cracked 31 homers in 1957.

Fast baller Dick Farrell, the Phillies' ace fireman in 1957 with a 10–2 record.

The young and the old of the Dodgers infield in 1957: Pee Wee Reese *(left)* and Charlie Neal.

Cubs right-hander Dick Drott, 15–11 in 1957. Just twenty-one years old, he had what looked like a fine career curtailed by a sore arm.

Dodger outfielder Gino Cimoli.

Frank Malzone, fine third baseman of the Boston Red Sox. He
drove in 103 runs in 1957.

Boston Red Sox shortstop Billy
Klaus.

Outfielder Harry Simpson. They
called him "Suitcase" because he
did a lot of packing and unpack-
ing, in the 1950s playing for the
Indians, Athletics, Yankees, Athletics again, White Sox, and Pirates. He led the American
League in triples in 1956 and
1957.

Boston's venerable Fenway Park, built in 1912.

Right-hander Harry Byrd, who pitched for the Athletics, Yankees, Orioles, White Sox, and Tigers in the 1950s.

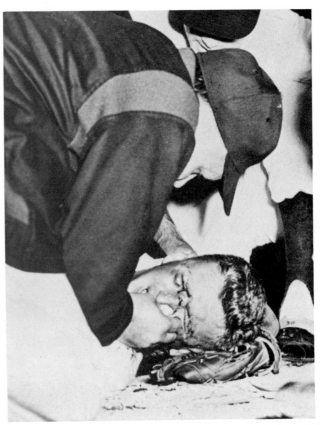

Herb Score, moments after being struck by Gil McDougald's line drive.

Ted Williams.

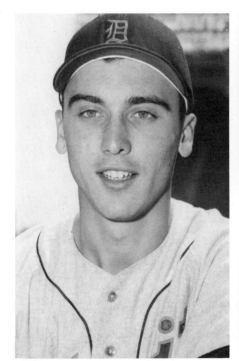

Detroit Tigers infielder Reno Bertoia.

Cincinnati Reds relief pitcher Tom Acker.

White Sox right-hander Bill Fischer.

Opposing managers in the 1957 World Series: the Yankees' Casey Stengel *(left)* and Milwaukee's Fred Haney.

Stan Musial.

1·9·5·8

Those who played against him in the opening weeks of the 1958 season said they had never seen anything like it. They all knew that Stan Musial was a great hitter—the Cardinal scorcher had been proving it for 15 years—but in the spring of 1958 he was hitting line drives that threatened to start grass fires when they struck the outfield. In the spring of 1958 Stanley Musial had a goal.

Musial had ended the 1957 season with a lifetime total of 2,957 hits, leaving him just 43 away from joining one of baseball's truly select groups. Since the beginning of organized ball in 1876, only seven men had accumulated 3,000 hits: Ty Cobb, Tris Speaker, Honus Wagner, Eddie Collins, Cap Anson, Nap Lajoie, and Paul Waner, the last to enter this lofty circle, 16 years before.

When the 1958 season began, Musial, the most modest and self-effacing of great hitters, went after his goal with a ferocity seldom seen at home plate. He opened the season with a 17-game hitting streak, during which he batted a sublime .529. It took him another 5 games—22 in all—to collect the 43 hits he needed. The landmark hit was a double at Wrigley Field on May 13. Then he went back to being the normal Stan Musial again, which meant a season's batting average of .337.

In 1957, the Milwaukee Braves won the pennant by eight games over the Cardinals; in 1958 they again won the pennant by eight games, this time over Danny Murtaugh's Pirates, a team beginning to see daylight after years of patient rebuilding.

The Braves were at or near the top all summer long, but at times they had considerable company. On July 4, the traditional midway point, Milwaukee was in first place, while the last-place Dodgers were just seven games out, making it the tightest July 4 package ever in the National League. But Fred Haney's team played the steadiest ball through the second half of the season and gradually pulled away from the persistent Pirates.

The Braves won despite injuries to three key players. Right-hander Bob Buhl, an 18-game winner the year before, missed most of the season with a sore arm and posted a 5–2 record. Outfielder Wes Covington's knee injuries limited him to 90 games, in which he hit 24 home runs, drove in 74 runs, and batted .330, while various ailments limited second baseman Red Schoendienst to 106 games.

The bulk of the pitching was handled by Warren Spahn (22–11) and Lew Burdette (20–10), with help from right-handers Bob Rush, Carl Willey, Joey Jay, and relief ace Don McMahon.

The rest of Haney's cast was familiar: Henry Aaron (30 home runs, .326), Eddie Mathews (31 homers), Johnny Logan, Del Crandall, Joe Adcock, Bill Bruton, and Frank Torre.

The Pirates now had in place the nucleus of the team that would be world champions in 1960: shortstop Dick Groat, second baseman Bill Mazeroski, and outfielders Bill Virdon, Bob Skinner, and Roberto Clemente, with Clemente flashing with greater consistency now the talents that would ultimately rank him among the game's all-time greats.

Pirate right-hander Bob Friend's 22 wins tied him with Spahn at the top of the league, while two other Pittsburgh righties, Vernon Law and reliever Roy Face, were getting better and better.

The transplanted Giants gave San Francisco a third-place finish. The club was headed by Willie Mays, who batted .347 in his new time zone, and by a brand-new slugger, Rookie of the Year Orlando Cepeda. The twenty-year-old first baseman was the genuine article—his .312 batting average, 25 home runs, and 96 runs batted in were simply a dust-up for bigger things to come. The Giants also introduced two more outstanding first-year men in third baseman Jim

1·9·5·8

Davenport and outfielder Felipe Alou.

Playing in Seals Stadium, with a seating capacity of under 23,000, the Giants vindicated their transcontinental hop by drawing 1,272,625 customers, nearly doubling the club's draw in the Polo Grounds the year before.

Cincinnati, which had averaged nearly 200 home runs a year over the previous three years, suddenly found itself rolling smaller cannons to the plate. Ted Kluszewski and Wally Post were gone in trades, while George Crowe hit just 7 homers, Gus Bell 10, and Ed Bailey 11. Only Frank Robinson had the range, hitting 31 of the team's 123 homers.

In Chicago, the story was Ernie Banks, exploding to the higher precincts of achievement with one of the greatest seasons of his ornamented career. The Cub shortstop, voted the league's Most Valuable Player, led the league with 47 home runs, 129 runs batted in, and a .614 slugging average, while batting .313. The Cubs were, in fact, the league's most lethal powder keg that year, hitting the most home runs, 182. In addition to Banks, four other Cubs hit 20 or more homers: outfielders Walt Moryn (26), Lee Walls (24), and Bobby Thomson (21) and first baseman Dale Long (20). The Cubs' bugaboo—again the old story—was pitching. Right-hander Glen Hobbie was the big winner with a 10–6 record.

The Dodgers prospered in Los Angeles, but it was at the box office and not on the field. An attendance of 1,845,556, exceeding the best the club had ever done in Brooklyn, lit up the front office, but on the field the team failed to acclimate. After 13 straight years of first-, second-, or third-place finishes, Walter Alston's club found itself blundering about in seventh place.

"The Brooklyns," as they were still referred to back East, just couldn't get squared away in the land of eternal sunshine. Their pitching, supposedly the strongest in the league, suffered the most. Longtime ace Don Newcombe opened up with an 0–6 record before being traded to the Reds. Carl Erskine had a sore arm. Don Drysdale, their young 17-game winner of 1957, found it difficult to adjust to pitching with a 251-foot left-field screen at his back.

"Drysdale's strength was pitching inside," Alston said. "In that park, with that left field, he was afraid to. So he changed his style of pitching, and it just didn't work for him." The big right-hander finished with a 12–13 record. Young Sandy Koufax, finally given the chance to work, was 11–11, gradually beginning to master the searing fast ball and curve that were soon to make him the brightest star in the baseball galaxy.

The Dodgers missed Roy Campanella (who had suffered his paralyzing automobile accident the previous January), while Gil Hodges swung a slower bat (just 22 homers in spite of the neighborly left-field screen), and Duke Snider, emasculated by the spacious right field, fell to 15 home runs after five straight years of 40 or more. Only Carl Furillo, with 18 homers and a .290 batting average, retained the numbers he was accustomed to posting in Brooklyn.

Philadelphia's Richie Ashburn won his second batting title by hitting .350, beating out Mays on the last day of the season. But while Robin Roberts won 17, 1957's 19-game-winning Rookie of the Year Jack Sanford fell to a 10–13 record. Despite a team batting average of .266, which tied the Braves for the league's best, the Phillies finished last for the eighteenth time in their history, more than any other National League club.

The American League continued on like a theatrical troupe that had an act that was too good to change: Casey Stengel first, Al Lopez second. That's the way it was again in 1958, for the seventh time in eight years as Casey's

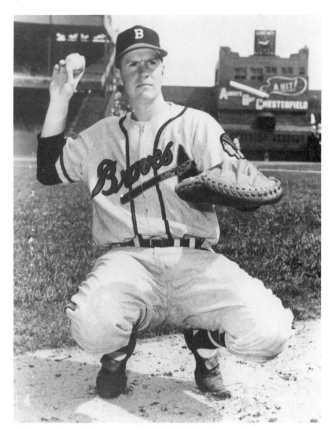

Milwaukee Braves catcher Del Crandall.

Milwaukee outfielder Wes Covington, who batted 330 in 1958.

Don McMahon, Milwaukee's ace reliever.

1·9·5·8

Yanks rolled to their ninth pennant in ten tries and Al, with the White Sox, brought up the immediate rear guard.

It was the Yankees' twenty-fourth pennant, a remarkable total, and more so when one realizes they didn't take their first until 1921. That was 24 pennants in 38 years, a run of success that gave the American League a Snow White and the Seven Dwarfs look.

The Yankees started the season as though shot from a cannon, while the other clubs took off like so many leaky water pistols. The New Yorkers won 7 of their first 8 and 25 of their first 31, and were in first place every day of the season.

By the beginning of August, the Yankees owned a 17-game lead over second-place Chicago. Stengel's club had been so dominant that no other team in the league had so much as a .500 record. (Chicago's .532 winning percentage, based on an 82–72 record, was the lowest ever for a second-place team.)

At that point the laws of probability, or maybe it was complacency, set in and the New Yorkers slumped enough for the White Sox to trim the deficit to 10½ games, when an irate Stengel locked the clubhouse and gave his players an angry readout. Properly chastised, the Yankee express rebalanced itself and headed for home, winning by ten.

While Mickey Mantle saw a drop in his batting average from .365 to .304, the Yankee cannoneer ripped 42 home runs to lead the league by one over Cleveland's Rocky Colavito. The Yankees had two other .300 hitters in Elston Howard and Norm Siebern.

On the mound, the Yankees had their first 20-game winner in four years. Fast-balling right-hander Bob Turley finally delivered the big season the club had been waiting for. In winning the Cy Young Award (the first American League pitcher to do so), Bullet Bob was 21–7, with 6 shutouts. The only other Yankee pitcher to break into double figures in the win column was Whitey Ford with a 14–7 record, with 7 shutouts and a 2.01 ERA, the last two figures being the best in the league. Ford would have done better, but arm trouble prevented him from winning another game after August 8. Arm miseries also restricted the effectiveness of Don Larsen (9–6) and Tom Sturdivant (3–6), but Stengel got sensational year-long relief pitching from an extremely hard-throwing right-hander named Ryne Duren. Peering through thick-lensed eyeglasses, and not known for pinpoint control, Duren was a terrifying figure on the mound. In 1958, his first year as a Yankee, he won 6 games and saved 20 others, striking out 87 in 76 innings.

The second-place White Sox hit the fewest homers (101) but stole the same amount of bases, and those 101 steals were more than double any other team's. Luis Aparicio with 29 swipes led the league for the third year in a row.

Teamed with Aparicio in the center of the White Sox diamond was slap hitter Nelson Fox at second base, picking up the most hits (187) and the fewest strikeouts (11). Leading in fewest whiffs was a Nelson Fox trademark, the White Sox pepperpot achieving it eleven times between 1951 and 1962, more than any player in history. In 1958, Fox set a record by going 98 games in a row without striking out, until Whitey Ford nailed him on August 23.

There were two no-hitters in the American League in 1958. The first was pitched by Detroit's Jim Bunning against the Red Sox on July 20, the second by Baltimore's knuckle baller Hoyt Wilhelm against the Yankees on September 20. But the best-pitched game of the year in the American League belonged to Chicago's Billy Pierce. Working against Washington on June 27, the White Sox southpaw came within a whisker of pitching baseball's first regular-season perfect game since another White Sox pitcher, Charley Robertson, had done it against Detroit in 1922. After retiring the first 26 batters he faced, Pierce gave up a double to pinch

1·9·5·8

hitter Ed Fitzgerald, the ball dropping just a foot fair inside the right-field foul line. Billy retired the next man and settled for one of the most glittering one-hitters ever pitched.

In 1957, Ted Williams had established a record by becoming at the age of thirty-nine the oldest man ever to win a batting title. In 1958, Williams reset his own record when he took his sixth and final batting crown. Though 60 points under his 1957 average, Ted's .328 was still good enough to be the best. In winning, Williams had to outshoot teammate Pete Runnels, who wound up at .322.

Another Red Sox bombardier, Jackie Jensen, hit 35 home runs and took the RBI title with 122, numbers that earned him the MVP award. With Williams, Runnels, Jensen, and Frank Malzone (.295), the Red Sox had four steady hitters in the lineup; but the rest of the Boston attack was diluted by three other regulars who demonstrated a curious low-grade consistency—first baseman Dick Gernert, shortstop Don Buddin, and outfielder Jimmy Piersall each batted .237.

The Tigers had good starting pitching in right-handers Frank Lary (16–15), Paul Foytack (15–13), and Jim Bunning (14–12), but the only real punch in the lineup belonged to their K-men, Harvey Kuenn and Al Kaline, who batted .319 and .313, respectively. Kuenn, a shortstop by trade but never particularly agile at the position, was switched to the outfield that year. Dividing the shortstop position for the Tigers were two men: Coot Veal and former Yankee second baseman Billy Martin. Martin, who was later to gain notoriety as a peripatetic manager who more often than not left behind ruffled feelings, apparently manifested the same wayward charm as a player. In 1957 he played for the Yankees and Athletics, in 1958 Detroit, in 1959 Cleveland, in 1960 Cincinnati, and in 1961 Milwaukee and Minnesota. Billy, it seems, was always Billy.

There wasn't much going on in Kansas City that year except for the booming bat of ex-Yankee outfielder Bob Cerv, who hit 38 home runs. Similarly, there wasn't much happening in Washington either, except for another booming bat. This one belonged to Roy Sievers, who hit 39 home runs. It all made for an interesting home run derby, which ended up like this: Mantle 42, Colavito 41, Sievers 39, Cerv 38. The last-place Senators also derived some solace from having the league's Rookie of the Year in Albie Pearson, a 5'6" outfielder who batted .275.

Baltimore also had a bit of home run glory to show. Gus Triandos's 30 homers tied him with Yogi Berra for the league record for most home runs by a catcher.

First baseman Vic Power, traded by Kansas City to Cleveland in June, was a steady hitter and one of the flashiest glovemen around. Power got into 93 games for Cleveland and stole just two bases. Why mention it? Well, because both were steals of home and both came in the same game against Detroit on August 14, the second coming in the tenth inning to give Cleveland the winning run. Power was the first American League player to steal home twice in a single game.

The World Series looked like another Milwaukee show—after four games. The Braves were up on the Yankees three games to one, but then Stengel's boys went to work and reclaimed their title by knocking over the Braves in the last three games. Leading the Yankee charge in those three games was Bob Turley, who polished off his Cy Young season with a win, a save, and a win. The Yankees were the first club since the 1925 Pirates to bounce back from a 1–3 deficit to win the World Series.

Henry Aaron.

Henry Aaron

Henry Aaron began his big-league career with the Milwaukee Braves in 1954, and by the time it was all over, in 1976 (when Henry was finishing up in Milwaukee, but this time in the American League with the Brewers), many of baseball's man-sized all-time records belonged to him, topmost among them the most haloed of lifetime achievements—755 home runs.

Aaron rang up all those home runs by swinging with a consistency that was most unusual for a power hitter. He was also most fortunate in that he was able to play out his long career virtually injury-free, playing in 150 or more games a season 14 times. From 1955 through 1970, he never played in fewer than 145 games.

Aaron was born in Mobile, Alabama, on February 5, 1934. A sandlot star in his hometown, he was signed by the Indianapolis Clowns of the Negro League while still a teenager. It was a good deal for the Clowns, as the youngster was spotted almost immediately by the Boston Braves, who gave the Clowns $10,000 for Henry.

Aaron entered organized ball in 1952 as a shortstop for the Eau Claire team in the Northern League, batted .336, and earned a promotion to Jacksonville in the South Atlantic League. Playing second base now, he batted .362 and the following year was a Milwaukee Brave.

Lacking the flamboyance of contemporaries Willie Mays and Roberto Clemente, Aaron was nonetheless their equal. He was a better hitter than either, as well as an excellent outfielder. For 20 years in a row he hit 20 or more home runs per season (a major-league record); 15 times he hit 30 or more home runs (a major-league record), and 8 times 40 or more (a National League record).

The record book, which might be subtitled *The Life and Times of Henry Aaron,* shows him scoring 100 or more runs 15 times, leading in total bases 8 times, 300 or more total bases 15 times, most extra base hits lifetime (1,477), most total bases lifetime (6,856), most runs batted in lifetime (2,297), and on and on, right up to his Cooperstown plaque.

Henry got into two World Series with the Braves in 1957 and 1958 and kept right on rapping, batting .393 in 1957 (with three home runs) and .333 in 1958. In the 1969 league championship series against the Mets he batted .357 with three homers in three games.

Aaron's talents were without limit. As a base stealer, he stole over 20 bases six times (unusual for a major home run hitter), and he would have done much better if his managers—fearful of a sliding injury—had turned him loose more often.

Along with his 755 home runs, Aaron collected a career total of 3,771 hits, third on the all-time rolls, behind Pete Rose and Ty Cobb.

The Giants' rookie slugger Orlando Cepeda.

Giants outfielder Felipe Alou, a rookie in 1958.

Outfielder Jerry Lynch, a .312 hitter for Cincinnati in 1958.

Brooks Robinson.

Cleveland first baseman Vic Power.

Jackie Jensen of the Red Sox, 1958's RBI leader in the American League.

Ted Williams, who won his sixth and final batting title in 1958 at the age of forty.

Red Sox shortstop Don Buddin.

Red Sox second baseman Pete Runnels, who batted .322 in 1958.

Athletics slugger Bob Cerv, who hit 38 home runs in 1958.
(Photo by Bob Olen.)

Washington right-hander Tex Clevenger.

Pittsburgh outfielder Bob Skinner, a .321 hitter in 1958.

Pittsburgh bopper Frank Thomas—35 homers in 1958.

Pittsburgh center fielder Bill Virdon.

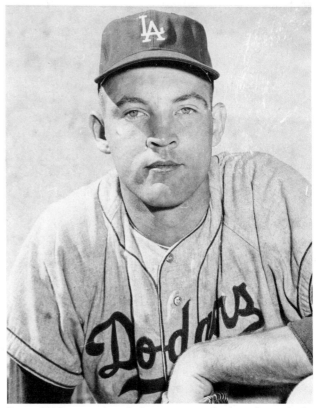

Stan Williams, hard-throwing right-hander of the Los Angeles Dodgers.

Billy O'Dell, talented southpaw of the Baltimore Orioles.

Ace of the Red Sox bullpen in 1958, Mike Fornieles.

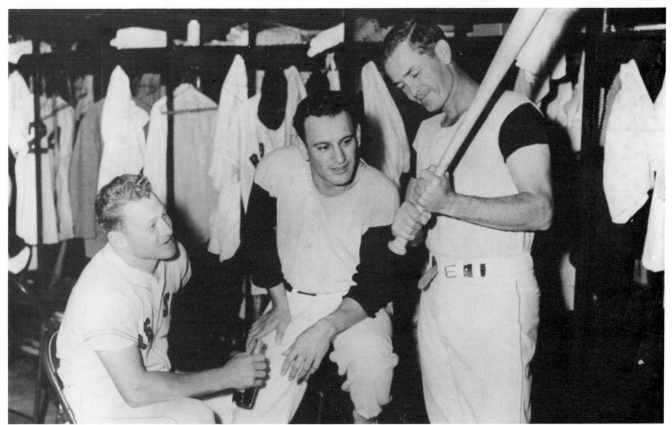

A high-level discussion of hitting in the Red Sox clubhouse. *Left to right:* Jackie Jensen, Frank Malzone, Pete Runnels.

There may have been a few as good but surely none better at shortstop than Cincinnati's Roy McMillan.

Sammy White, the Red Sox' regular catcher through the 1950s.

Pittsburgh's Forbes Field.

Don Blasingame, second baseman of the St. Louis Cardinals.

The Chicago White Sox' utility infielder Sam Esposito.

Jim Davenport, the Giants' sure-handed third baseman.

Leading the National League with 69 appearances in 1958 was Chicago Cubs reliever Don Elston.

Pittsburgh's 22-game-winning Bob Friend.

The Yankees' Bob Turley, 1958's Cy Young Award winner. *(Photo by Bob Olen.)*

Willie Mays of the San Francisco Giants. Willie hit .347 in his first year on the West Coast.

Yankee reliever Ryne Duren, one of the hardest throwers of his time. *(Photo by Bob Olen.)*

Curt Flood, the Cardinals' gifted ball-hawking center fielder.

Milwaukee first baseman Frank Torre. He batted .309 in 1958.

Bob Purkey, Cincinnati right-hander who was 17–11 in 1958.

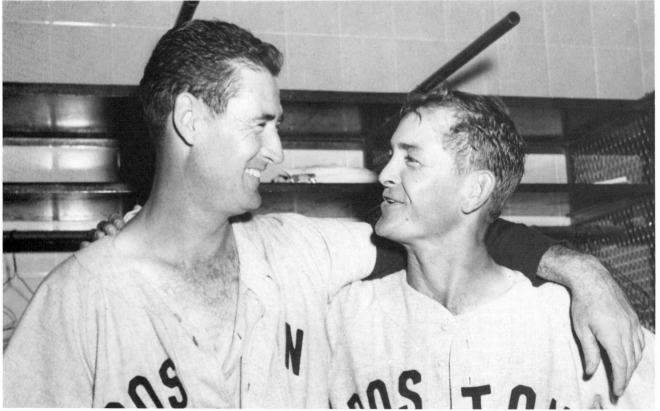

Ted Williams (left) and Pete Runnels, whom Ted edged out for the batting crown in 1958, .328 to .322.

Kansas City A's right-hander Ray Herbert.

After pitching for the Giants and Dodgers, Sal Maglie completed the New York cycle by pitching for the Yankees.

The season is long over and snow is falling in the silence of Fenway Park.

Gil Hodges has just scored the winning run in the bottom of the twelfth inning of the second Dodgers-Braves playoff game to give Los Angeles the pennant. The flying objects are jackets thrown jubilantly from the Dodger dugout.

1·9·5·9

Suddenly the Southern California climate agreed with the Dodgers. Recovering from their seventh-place shakedown cruise in 1958, Walter Alston's transplants took an express elevator all the way to the top in 1959, but not before going through a sizzling three-way fight with the Braves and Giants.

On the morning of the season's final day there existed the mathematical possibility of a three-way tie, if the Giants won their doubleheader and the Dodgers and Braves lost their single games.

The Braves, heavy preseason favorites to take a third straight pennant, got off to a fast start and set the pace up to the All-Star break. At that point, only 3½ games separated the top four clubs—Milwaukee, San Francisco, Los Angeles, and Pittsburgh. The Pirates suffered an 11–16 July tailspin that effectively removed them from the chase.

On July 9, the Giants took over the top spot, and they held on to it for most of the remainder of the season, not letting go until the decisive final days.

On September 14, just one game separated the Braves, Giants, and Dodgers. On September 17, the Giants held a two-game lead over their pursuers with just eight left to play. On September 19, the Dodgers beat the Giants twice in a day-night doubleheader and the chase became grim as the lead changed hands seven times in the next nine days.

On the final day, the Giants lost their doubleheader while the Dodgers and Braves, in a dead heat, each won their game, necessitating a best-two-of-three playoff. It was the third pennant playoff in National League history, and each had featured the Dodgers—losers to St. Louis in 1946 and New York in 1951. Los Angeles fans were getting a full dose of what Brooklyn fans had for years been subjected to—watching their heroes in breathtaking hand-to-hand combat at season's end.

The Dodgers won the first game, played at Milwaukee, 3–2, thanks to 7⅔ innings of blazing shutout ball hurled by relief pitcher Larry Sherry. The winning run was a home run by catcher John Roseboro in the sixth inning.

As if determined not to do things the easy way, the Dodgers put themselves and their fans through the wringer the following day in Los Angeles. Going into the bottom of the ninth the Braves seemed to have things well in hand, leading 5–2 with 21-game winner Lew Burdette on the mound. The Dodgers, however, rallied for three runs to tie the game. It went on for three more tension-filled innings until the Dodgers won it in the bottom of the twelfth, 6–5.

Unlike the Dodger teams back in Brooklyn, this one was not a collection of overachievers. Winners of just 88 games (including the 2 in the playoff), the lowest number for a pennant winner in National League history (the 1918 Cubs won fewer in a season shortened by the war), the Dodgers received solid efforts rather than spectacular ones. Duke Snider led the team with a .308 batting average and just 88 runs batted in, while Wally Moon, acquired from the Cardinals over the winter, batted .302. Gil Hodges, second baseman Charlie Neal, third baseman Jim Gilliam, and utility man Norm Larker also gave the club a summer of good and steady work.

Don Drysdale, gradually overcoming the trauma of pitching in the Coliseum, led the staff with a 17–13 record. The big right-hander's 242 strikeouts were the best in the league, helping the Dodger pitching staff lead the league in whiffs for the twelfth straight year with a new major-league record of 1,077 (the Los Angeles mound corps would go on to top the league in strikeouts for the next four years, making it sixteen in a row, before finally being bypassed by the Cincinnati staff in 1964).

The Braves had two of the league's 20-game winners, Spahn and Burdette, each with a 21–

1·9·5·9

15 mark. Bob Buhl was 15–9 and Don McMahon was first-rate in the bullpen, but the Braves did not get the help they were expecting from Joey Jay and Carl Willey, who together logged an 11–20 record.

Milwaukee received the usual big years from sluggers Henry Aaron and Eddie Mathews. Eddie led the league with 46 home runs, drove in 114 runs, and batted .306; Henry hit 39 homers, drove in 123 runs, led with 223 hits, and won his second batting crown with a .355 average. Joe Adcock hit 25 homers and Del Crandall 21, but the club sorely missed the presence of second baseman Red Schoendienst, who was out virtually the entire season after contracting tuberculosis. The Braves employed seven second baseman during the season, none of whom came close to doing an adequate job.

The Giants blew the pennant when they lost 11 of their last 16 games. Bill Rigney's four starters, who started 135 games, simply ran out of gas before they could cover those final miles. Right-hander Sam Jones, who started 35 games and relieved in 15 others, was 21–15, Johnny Antonelli was 19–10, Jack Sanford 15–12, and lefty McCormick 12–16.

The Giants featured some of the league's best hitting, led by Willie Mays (34 homers, 104 runs batted in, .313) and Orlando Cepeda (27 homers, 105 RBIs, .317). Later in the season they were joined by the eventual Rookie of the Year, Willie McCovey. Breaking into 52 games, the twenty-year-old McCovey, possessor of one of the sweetest power swings ever seen, began his Hall of Fame career with 13 home runs and a .354 batting average.

Pittsburgh relief pitcher Roy Face turned in one of the most astonishing year-long performances ever by a reliever. The five-foot-eight-inch fork baller won his first 17 decisions before finally being stopped by the Dodgers on September 11, finishing with an 18–1 card.

Face's 17 straight wins fell two short of the one-season record of 19 set by the Giants' Rube Marquard in 1912.

Chicago's Ernie Banks became the first National Leaguer to win back-to-back Most Valuable Player awards. The Cubs' shortstop did it on the strength of 45 home runs and 143 runs batted in. Ernie was the whole show in Chicago that year, no other Cub hitting more than 14 homers or driving in more than 52 runs.

The Reds, finishing in a fifth-place tie with the Cubs, scored the most runs (764) and had the highest team figures in batting (.274) and slugging (.427), but saw themselves undone by their pitching. The best their two big winners—Don Newcombe and Bob Purkey—could do was 13 apiece. At bat, the club had a trio of .300 hitters in Frank Robinson (.311, with 36 homers and 125 RBIs), Johnny Temple (.311), and outfielder Vada Pinson (.316). Playing his first full season, the twenty-year-old Pinson was launching what was going to be a long and productive career.

In St. Louis, the erosions of time were beginning to show on Stan Musial, as the thirty-eight-year-old great batted just .255, his first dip under .300 after 16 straight years over that significant dividing line.

Cardinal third baseman Ken Boyer batted .309 and hit 28 home runs. Boyer also had the major leagues' longest consecutive-game hitting streak since Musial's 30 in 1950. From August 10 through September 12, Boyer hit in 29 straight games. The Cards also received fine years from a couple of players who each split their time between the outfield and first base. Joe Cunningham batted .345 and Bill White .302.

There were two outstanding individual pitching performances in the league that year. On August 31, Los Angeles' Sandy Koufax set a new National League record when he fanned 18 Giants, breaking by one Dizzy Dean's 1933

1·9·5·9

record, and tying Bob Feller's major-league high. Starting with one out in the fourth inning, Koufax registered 15 of his last 17 outs via whiffs. He kept getting stronger right to the end, fanning the side in the ninth on ten pitches. A three-run homer by Wally Moon in the bottom of the ninth gave Koufax a 5–2 win.

The other pitching highlight of the year was turned in by Pittsburgh southpaw Harvey Haddix, and it was destined to become one of the landmark mound performances in all of baseball history. After a 20-game rookie year in 1953, Haddix had been a steady albeit unspectacular pitcher. By 1959 he was working his way toward the respectable oblivion of the .500 pitcher. But suddenly, on the night of May 26, he turned in the greatest single-game achievement ever by a pitcher.

Pitching against the hard-hitting Braves in Milwaukee (whose lineup included Henry Aaron, Eddie Mathews, Joe Adcock, Wes Covington, Del Crandall, and Andy Pafko), Haddix hooked up with Lew Burdette. For 12 innings neither pitcher allowed a run. But while Burdette was scattering 12 singles, Harvey was giving up nothing, absolutely nothing: not a hit, not a walk, not a naked bone, not a thing. With his teammates playing flawlessly behind him, Haddix pitched 12 perfect innings—36 Braves up, 36 down. No other pitcher in history had ever gone more than 9 innings in a game without allowing a base runner, nor had any ever pitched more than 10⅔ hitless innings in a single game. On that night Haddix broke both these records, and with something to spare, as he pitched the most elegant game in major-league history.

In the thirteenth inning, however, he lost.

After Burdette, pitching with less distinction but equal tenacity, had retired the Pirates in the top of the inning, Milwaukee leadoff man Felix Mantilla was safe when third baseman Don Hoak picked up his grounder and threw low to first base. Eddie Mathews sacrificed Mantilla to second. Aaron was intentionally walked.

Haddix still had his no-hitter and his shutout, but both were about to be wiped away. Joe Adcock caught hold of one and drove it over the fence. There was some base-path confusion when Aaron thought the ball hit the fence; Adcock passed Henry on the base line, nullifying the home run, but Mantilla scored. It was recorded as a 1–0 Milwaukee victory. Burdette won—a 13-inning shutout—but Haddix went as eminently into the record books as it was possible for a pitcher to go on the strength of one day's work.

In what one hopes is an apocryphal story, it was reported that after the game a young writer asked the unhappy Haddix, "Harvey, is this the best game you ever pitched?" It was also reported, though never confirmed, that a few days later Haddix received a letter signed by a few dozen members of a college fraternity that read, in its entirety:

Dear Harvey:
Tough shit.

If not for Al Lopez, the American League would have been put into a near-permanent state of embarrassment, for if Al's Indians in 1954 and White Sox in 1959 had not won pennants, then the New York Yankees would have taken every American League pennant from 1949 through 1964.

On May 20, in fact, baseball fans found out how unexpectedly the world could be turned upside down when a glance at the standings showed Casey Stengel's perennials—winners of nine of the last ten pennants—resting sullenly and uncomfortably in last place. The New Yorkers remained there until the end of the month. It took an 18–12 June to move them back into contention. In July, the Red Sox had the satisfying—and extremely rare—experience of administering five straight defeats to the Yan-

Harvey Haddix pitching to Milwaukee's Eddie Mathews during the historic game on May 26 in which Haddix pitched 12 perfect innings before losing 1–0.

Roy Face, Pittsburgh's crack relief pitcher, who was 18–1 in 1959.

1·9·5·9

kees at Fenway Park, a pasting from which the world champs seemed never to recover. At season's end, the Yankees were in third place, 15 games behind the White Sox and 10 behind second-place Cleveland. (Those who thought the Yankee dynasty had finally come to a halt were in for a long and dismaying dose of reality—starting the next season, the New Yorkers reeled off another five pennants in a row.)

The race was between Lopez's White Sox and Joe Gordon's Indians—Cleveland power versus Chicago speed and pitching. The Chicagoans were known as the "Go-Go Sox" because of their relentless hustle and spirit, much of which came from second baseman and Most Valuable Player Nelson Fox. At .306, Fox was the club's only .300 hitter. Catcher Sherman Lollar, with 22 home runs, was the only legitimate power threat.

Luis Aparicio stole 56 bases for the scampering Sox, an unusually high number for those years, while continuing to write the book at shortstop. In center field, the Sox had one of the best gloves at that position in Jim Landis, but Jim hit just five home runs and batted .272. Right fielder Al Smith batted .237, first baseman Earl Torgeson .220, third baseman Bubba Phillips .264, Aparicio .257. With stats like that on a pennant winner, you look to the pitching staff, and here the view is more pleasing.

The ace of Lopez's staff was one of his big men from his Cleveland days, Early Wynn, now thirty-nine years old and delivering his last truly big season. "Burly Early" was 22–10, good enough to carry off the Cy Young Award. Behind him were righty Bob Shaw (18–6), Billy Pierce (14–15), and a bullpen tandem of veteran right-handers Gerry Staley and Turk Lown (who came by his nickname legitimately: his given name was Omar). Between them, Staley and Lown made 127 appearances, winning 17 and saving 29.

Cleveland, lacking the strong pitching of previous years, tried to do it with muscle. Rocky Colavito busted 42 home runs and drove in 111 of his mates. Woodie Held, who played infield and outfield, hit 29 boomers, Minnie Minoso had 21, and Tito Francona 20. Francona, who got into 122 games, batted .363 (falling short, however, of qualifying for the batting title).

Right-hander Cal McLish led the Cleveland staff with a fine 19–8 record. (He also led all of baseball in names, his full handle being Calvin Coolidge Julius Caesar Tuskahoma McLish. His teammates called him "Buster.") The Indians also had righties Gary Bell (16–11), Jim Perry (12–10), and Jim Grant (10–7). Herb Score, trying to make it back, was 9–11.

The season pivoted on a four-game Indian–White Sox series at the end of August, played in Cleveland. The Indians had run off eight straight wins and pulled to within one game of Lopez's club. This year, however, Al was not going to settle for second place. In a stunning sweep that put a permanent chill into the Indians, the visiting White Sox took all four games and rolled in at the end with a five-game lead.

In showing how to take a pennant without any Goliaths in the lineup, the White Sox hit the major leagues' lowest number of homers (97), but they also had the lowest ERA (3.29), most stolen bases (113), and highest fielding percentage (.979). "They won it the old-fashioned way," said Baltimore skipper Paul Richards. They also won it by beating the two clubs they had to. The White Sox were 15–7 with Cleveland and 13–9 with New York. It was the first time since 1925 that a White Sox club had taken a season series from a Yankee club.

In New York, things just didn't go right. Some people cited the law of averages; but if there had ever been such a law it had been repealed a long time ago, or the Yankees wouldn't have taken nine of the last ten pennants. Those with a more realistic view of things pointed to the loss of Bill Skowron with a broken wrist for the second half of the season (Bill's replacement

1·9·5·9

was a big first baseman up from the minors named Marv Throneberry), and the ineffectiveness of right-handers Bob Turley (8–11) and Don Larsen (6–7). Whitey Ford at 16–10 was the top winner, but for Whitey it constituted an off year. The Yankees did get winning years from righties Duke Maas (14–8) and Art Ditmar (13–9), but it wasn't enough.

Also falling off considerably was Mickey Mantle, who dropped to a .285 batting average and just 75 runs batted in, unusually low for a man who hit 31 home runs. Only second baseman Bobby Richardson, at .301, scaled the .300 mark for the Yankees. The team's 687 runs was their lowest since 1946.

The Tigers had three 17-game winners in lefty Don Mossi and Frank Lary and Jim Bunning, plus the league's two top hitters in Harvey Kuenn (.353) and Al Kaline (.327), and Charlie Maxwell's 31 homers, but all it netted was fourth place.

The Red Sox had the RBI leader in Jackie Jensen (112), but little else. Fenway fans even had to endure the sight of Ted Williams batting .254, one of baseball's eye-rubbing statistics. With Stan Musial batting .255 for the Cardinals, it seemed that the roots of baseball's two long-time sequoias were starting to come loose. Coming to bat just 272 times, the forty-one-year-old Theodore hit only ten home runs. Many people thought the greatest hitter of them all had stayed at the fair one year too many, but he was to come back for one last hard-hitting season in 1960.

Baltimore manager Paul Richards made a starter out of veteran reliever Hoyt Wilhelm that year, and the knuckle baller was 15–11 with the league's best ERA, 2.19.

Kansas City had a twenty-four-year-old outfielder named Roger Maris, who hit 16 home runs but whose left-hand stroke was attractive to the Yankees, who acquired him in a postseason trade. It was one of many trades engineered by these two clubs in the second half of the

1950s as Kansas City kept feeding its best players to the Yankees in a series of swaps that became scandalous. In 1959, the Yankee roster included such former Athletics as Clete Boyer, Hector Lopez, Ralph Terry, Duke Maas, Art Ditmar, Ryne Duren, and Bobby Shantz. The Athletics' roster—counting players who came and went—included 20 either former or future Yankees.

The reason for these deals—most of them lopsided in favor of the Yankees—has never been made entirely clear. One theory had the Kansas City owner, Arnold Johnson, sharing business interests with Yankee co-owner Del Webb that made Johnson either beholden or at least compliant. Another explanation for the ceaseless traffic between New York and Kansas City was more prosaic—the K.C. people were gullible.

Finishing last for the third year in a row, the Washington Senators derived some measure of satisfaction by bringing up the Rookie of the Year for the second year in a row. His name was Bob Allison, and the young outfielder proved to be a robust slugger. He hit 30 home runs in his debut year, teaming with Jim Lemon, who hit 33, Roy Sievers, who hit 21, and the suddenly erupting young strong man from Idaho, Harmon Killebrew, who tied Colavito for the league lead with 42 home runs. That was a lot of thunder, but it couldn't roar them out of the cellar, which the club helped cinch with an 18-game losing streak (third worst in league history) from mid-July through early August.

There were a couple of high-caliber individual home run–hitting performances during the season. The first belonged to Detroit's Charlie Maxwell. On May 3, Charlie hit four consecutive home runs in a doubleheader against the Yankees at Detroit's Briggs Stadium. Charlie's first came in the seventh inning of the opener, and then in the second game he homered in his first three official times at bat. Max-

1·9·5·9

well was only the fifth American Leaguer to hit four home runs in a doubleheader and the sixth major leaguer to hit four straight home runs in two games.

An even more impressive fireworks display was put on by Cleveland's Rocky Colavito in Baltimore's Memorial Stadium on June 10. Going off like a row of hand grenades, Rocky connected for four straight home runs, becoming only the second American League player (Lou Gehrig in 1932 was the other) to hit four homers in a nine-inning game. Making Colavito's achievement even more impressive was the fact that he did it in what was considered to be baseball's toughest home run park. Since the Orioles began playing there in 1954, no *team* had ever hit more than three home runs in a single game in Memorial Stadium.

Early in the season, on April 22, there occurred one of the all-time oddball innings ever seen in major-league baseball. On that day, the White Sox scored 11 runs in the seventh inning against the Athletics on just one hit. Three Kansas City pitchers, Tom Gorman, Mark Freeman, and George Brunet, served up ten walks and hit a batter, while the rest of the club added to the generosity with three errors. The final score was Chicago 20, Kansas City 6.

On July 21, 1959, infielder Pumpsie Green broke into the Red Sox lineup and thereby brought to completion a revolutionary process that had begun 12 years earlier. Pumpsie, a black, had integrated the Boston Red Sox, baseball's last all-white roster. Why it had taken the Red Sox a dozen years to defer to reality and accept the inevitable is anyone's guess, and none of the guesses can be flattering to anyone.

Following is a list of the first black player with each team and the date of his first game:

Dodgers: Jackie Robinson, April 15, 1947
Indians: Larry Doby, July 5, 1947
Browns: Henry Thompson, July 17, 1947
Giants: Henry Thompson, July 8, 1949
Braves: Sam Jethroe, April 18, 1950
White Sox: Sam Hairston, July 21, 1951
Athletics: Bob Trice, September 13, 1953
Cubs: Ernie Banks, September 17, 1953
Pirates: Curt Roberts, April 13, 1954
Cardinals: Tom Alston, April 13, 1954
Reds: Saturnino Escalera, April 17, 1954
Senators: Carlos Paula, September 6, 1954
Yankees: Elston Howard, April 14, 1955
Phillies: John Kennedy, April 22, 1957
Tigers: Ossie Virgil, June 6, 1958
Red Sox: Pumpsie Green, July 21, 1959

The first California World Series saw the Dodgers bring a world championship to the West Coast by defeating the White Sox in six games. Relief pitcher Larry Sherry starred for the Dodgers, winning two games and saving two. The Los Angeles Coliseum may have been a bizarre place in which to play baseball, but it was also a very large one—the third, fourth, and fifth games of the Series were played there, and each drew over 92,000 customers.

Warren Spahn.

Warren Spahn

When he was a rookie pitcher for the Boston Braves in 1942, the twenty-one-year-old Warren Spahn was being warmed up by catcher Ernie Lombardi. One of Spahn's fast balls ranged outside; instead of shifting his feet to catch it, Lombardi reached out with his enormous bare right hand and snatched the ball out of the air.

"I put my hands on my hips and stared down at him," Spahn recalled. "I told myself that if he could catch my fast ball with his bare hand, then it just wasn't fast enough and I'd have to come up with another pitch."

Spahn came up with another pitch—several of them, in fact, including a screwball and an array of other breaking pitches, all of which he changed speeds on and delivered with meticulous control and with a motion so fluid and graceful that he became known as "poetry in motion."

Spahn, who was born in Buffalo, New York, on April 23, 1921, stands very high in a most impressive pitching category—his 363 wins rank him fifth on the all-time list, behind Cy Young, Walter Johnson, Grover Cleveland Alexander, and Christy Mathewson, and first among left-handers.

Making his win total all the more remarkable is the fact that Spahn didn't win his first big-league game until he came out of the service in 1946, at the age of twenty-five. After that it was one high-digit victory season after another, from 1947 through 1963, when he finally began to slow down, retiring in 1965.

Spahn possessed what must have been one of the most phenomenal arms ever to deliver a baseball. There is no record of his ever having a sore arm through 21 years and over 5,000 innings of work. From 1947 through 1963 he never started fewer than 32 games a year or worked less than 245 innings, leading the league in complete games nine times, seven times consecutively.

Perhaps Spahn's most notable accomplishment is his winning 20 or more games 13 times, equaling the record set by Mathewson. Through the 1950s, he was a 20-game winner eight times. His 63 career shutouts rank him sixth in that category.

Spahn led in victories eight times, earned-run average three times, strikeouts four times, and shutouts four times. He spent his entire career with the Braves, except for his final 1965 season, which he split between the New York Mets and San Francisco Giants.

He pitched a no-hitter against the Phillies in 1960, and a year later, at the age of forty, delivered another one against the Giants.

Spahn also helped himself in other ways. His pick-off move to first base was one of the most deceptive in baseball; also, he could swing the bat—his 35 lifetime home runs are the most by any pitcher in National League history.

Cleveland's Rocky Colavito
hit 42 homers in 1959.

Frank Robinson, who had 36 home runs in 1959.

On the brink of superstardom: Roberto Clemente.

Early Wynn, ace of the staff of the Chicago White Sox pennant winners in 1959 with a 22–10 record.

Chicago White Sox skipper Al Lopez.

White Sox third baseman Bubba Phillips.

White Sox right-hander Bob Shaw. He was 18–6 for the 1959 American League pennant winners.

White Sox relief specialist Turk Lown who was 9–2 with 15 saves in 1959.

Jim Landis of the White Sox, one of the fine center fielders in the American League.

Right-hander Dick Donovan of the White Sox.

Bill Veeck *(left)* and Hank Greenberg, president and vice-president, respectively, of the Chicago White Sox.

Sherman Lollar, the White Sox' solid man behind the plate in 1959.

Don Drysdale, the Dodgers' top winner in 1959 with 17.

Sandy Koufax, just 8–6 in 1959, but with 173 strikeouts in 153 innings.

Dodger outfielder Chuck Essegian, who created a stir by pinch-hitting two home runs in the 1959 World Series.

Dodger relief pitcher Larry Sherry.

Dodger first baseman—outfielder Norm Larker.

Willie McCovey, the Giants' Rookie of the Year in 1959.

Maury Wills, a rookie shortstop for the Dodgers in 1959.

Dodger catcher John Roseboro.

New York Yankee second baseman Bobby Richardson.

Yankee right-hander Art Ditmar.

Willie Mays.

San Francisco right-hander Jack Sanford.

Sam Jones, the Giants' ace in 1959 with a 21–15 record.

Mike McCormick, southpaw of the San Francisco Giants.

Bill White of the Cardinals, who alternated between first base and the outfield in 1959, batting .302.

Pittsburgh first baseman Dick Stuart found the home run range 27 times in 1959.

Cardinal outfielder–first baseman Joe Cunningham, who batted .345 in 1959.

Pirate ace Vernon Law, 18–9 in 1959.

Washington right-hander Camilo Pascual, winner of 17 games for a last-place team.

Washington Senators boomer Harmon Killebrew, who hit 42 home runs in 1959, tying Rocky Colavito for the league lead.

Washington's Rookie of the Year, outfielder Bob Allison, who hit 30 homers in 1959.

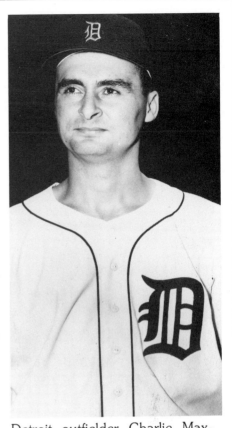

Outfielder Norm Siebern. The Yankees sent him to Kansas City as part of the deal for Roger Maris. *(Photo by Bob Olen.)*

Cal McLish of the Indians, 19–8 in 1959.

Detroit outfielder Charlie Maxwell. He had 31 homers in 1959.

Cincinnati's brilliant young outfielder, Vada Pinson, who collected 205 hits and batted .316 in his first full season.

Milwaukee's hard-throwing young left-hander, Juan Pizarro.

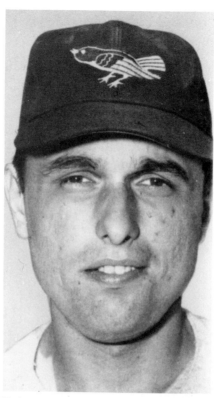

Pumpsie Green of the Red Sox.

Baltimore Orioles right-hander Milt Pappas, just twenty years old in 1959, with a 15–9 record.

Outfielder Tito Francona of the Indians, who batted .363 in 1959, but fell short of qualifying for the batting title.

Vic Wertz, one of the American League's fine sluggers through the 1950s, playing for Detroit, St. Louis, Baltimore, Cleveland, and Boston.

Jerry Lumpe of the Athletics, one of the many players who rode the shuttle between New York and Kansas City in the latter half of the 1950s.

Cleveland infielder Woodie Held, who hit 29 homers in 1959.

Chicago Cubs right-hander Glen Hobbie, 16–13 in 1959.

Right-hander Johnny Kucks, another passenger on the New York–Kansas City shuttle.

This young Philadelphia Phillies second baseman batted just .218 in 1959 in his one and only year as a big-league player But Sparky Anderson would be back, for a long and successful career as a manager.

Index